Two paintings on silk depicting Dejima Island, a view from the Bay (top), a view from Nagasaki (bottom), circa 1860 following Kawahara Keiga, paintings of Deshima Island, circa 1815.

Edward R. Tufte

Envisioning Information

Graphics Press   •   *Cheshire, Connecticut*

PUBLISHED BY GRAPHICS PRESS LLC
POST OFFICE BOX 430, CHESHIRE, CONNECTICUT 06410
WWW.TUFTE.COM

Printed in the United States of America   *Fourteenth printing, December 2013*

Contents

ESCAPING FLATLAND   12

MICRO/MACRO READINGS   37

LAYERING AND SEPARATION   53

SMALL MULTIPLES   67

COLOR AND INFORMATION   81

NARRATIVES OF SPACE AND TIME   97

EPILOGUE   121

for my teacher, Inge Druckrey

for my parents, Edward E. Tufte and Virginia James Tufte

and for Moshe, Tanya, Charlie, Natasha, Babar, and Frida

Introduction

THE world is complex, dynamic, multidimensional; the paper is static, flat. How are we to represent the rich visual world of experience and measurement on mere flatland?

This book celebrates escapes from flatland, rendering several hundred superb displays of complex data. Revealed here are design strategies for enhancing the dimensionality and density of portrayals of information—techniques exemplified in maps, the manuscripts of Galileo, timetables, notation describing dance movements, aerial photographs, the Vietnam Veterans Memorial, electrocardiograms, drawings of Calder and Klee, computer visualizations, and a textbook of Euclid's geometry.

Our investigation yields general principles that have specific visual consequences, governing the design, editing, analysis, and critique of data representations. These principles help to identify and to explain design excellence—why some displays are better than others.

Charts, diagrams, graphs, tables, guides, instructions, directories, and maps comprise an enormous accumulation of material. Once described by Philip Morrison as "cognitive art," it embodies tens of trillions of images created and multiplied the world over every year. Despite the beauty and utility of the best work, design of information has engaged little critical or aesthetic notice: there is no Museum of Cognitive Art. This book could serve as a partial catalog for such a collection. Like my previous study, *The Visual Display of Quantitative Information*, which derives theoretical counsel from the classics of statistical graphics, this book arrays exemplary designs—this time over a broader spectrum, for all types of information.

To envision information—and what bright and splendid visions can result—is to work at the intersection of image, word, number, art. The instruments are those of writing and typography, of managing large data sets and statistical analysis, of line and layout and color. And the standards of quality are those derived from visual principles that tell us how to put the right mark in the right place.

Finally, in reading the words and drawings, note that:

Many of the illustrations have been edited and redrawn (as indicated in the citations) in order to repair battered originals, to make new color separations, and to improve the design. Primary sources—the themes for my variations—are always noted.

The illustrations repay *careful* study. They are treasures, complex and witty, rich with meaning. The text, I do hope, is of similar character, with every word meant to count; all in all, the reader should proceed most slowly through these bountiful and condensed pages.

The principles of information design are universal—like mathematics— and are not tied to unique features of a particular language or culture. Consequently, our examples are widely distributed in space and time: illustrations come from 17 countries and 7 centuries, and, for that matter, 3 planets and 1 star.

Acknowledgments

I am most thankful for access to these libraries: in London, The British Library, and British Patent Office Library. In Paris, Bibliothèque Nationale, and Bibliothèque de l'Ecole Nationale des Ponts et Chaussées. In Tokyo, Arisugawa Memorial Park Library, and Japanese National Railroad Library. In the United States, the Library of Congress, New York Public Library at Lincoln Center, and, at Yale University, the Art and Architecture Library, Astronomy Library, Beinecke Rare Book and Manuscript Library, Center for British Art, Historical Medical Library, Social Science Library, Sterling Memorial Library, and especially Interlibrary Loan.

Original film separations for several maps and drawings were generously provided by Samuel Antupit of Harry N. Abrams, Inc.; Gary Graham, IBM Corporation; David Monahan, Marine Cartography, Canadian Hydrographic Service; M. Roggli, Bundesamt für Landestopographie, Wabern, Switzerland; Paul A. Tukey, Bell Communications Research; Wild Leitz, Ltd., Heerbrugg, Switzerland; and the Statistics Bureau, Prime Minister's Office, Japan.

At Yale University, I am blessed with students who often listen sympathetically and then go on to make their own independent contributions. Three drawings here are adapted from student work.

In this complex project, many have provided advice and assistance. I remember gratefully:

For finding (and selling) rare books and maps, Teresa Bridgeman, Jonathan Hill, Gordon Hollis, George N. Johnson, Jr., and Richard Lan.

For their patient guidance in exploring Japanese information design, Akiko Hashimoto, Fumihiko Saito, and the essential Nagayo Sawa.

For suggesting and contributing examples, Scott Adams, Robert Cameron, Inge Druckrey, Elisabeth Fairman, Gretchen Garner, Owen Gingerich, Howard I. Gralla, David H. Hathaway, Nicholas Johnson, Herbert A. Klein, Paul Levy, Pamela Pfeffer, Denise Scott Brown, Ani Stern, Vane Sutton-Vane, R. Gay Walker, Colin Ware, Jon Wertheimer, Berthold Wolpe.

For reviewing the manuscript, Rudolf Arnheim, Samuel Edgerton, Jr., Joanna Hitchcock, Virgina J. Tufte, and Kim Veltman; and for helpful advice, Robert K. Merton.

For elegant book design and counsel for many years, Howard I. Gralla; for typesetting in Monotype Bembo, Michael and Winifred Bixler; for advice on an intricate printing job, Don Dehoff, William Glick, and Robert Hennessey; for vigilant production review, Carolyn Williams.

For managing Graphics Press with special care, Elaine Lau and Kathy Orlando; and for managing the rest, Cynthia Bill.

For superb and reflective research support, Scott Adams and Mark Hansen.

For fine craft in artwork, and redrawing and adapting many of the examples, Nora Hillman Goeler.

For her ideas and inspiration, Inge Druckrey.

January 1990
Cheshire, Connecticut

1   *Escaping Flatland*

EVEN though we navigate daily through a perceptual world of three spatial dimensions and reason occasionally about higher dimensional arenas with mathematical ease, the world portrayed on our information displays is caught up in the two-dimensionality of the endless flatlands of paper and video screen.[1] All communication between the readers of an image and the makers of an image must now take place on a two-dimensional surface. *Escaping this flatland is the essential task of envisioning information—for all the interesting worlds (physical, biological, imaginary, human) that we seek to understand are inevitably and happily multivariate in nature. Not flatlands.*

[1] The idea of "flatland" is based on the classic by A. Square [Edwin A. Abbott], *Flatland: A Romance of Many Dimensions* (London, 1884). A recent statement from an artist's viewpoint (How can modern painting, abstractionism, escape flatland?) is found in Frank Stella, *Working Space* (Cambridge, 1986).

THIS chapter outlines a variety of design strategies that sharpen the information resolution, the resolving power, of paper and video screen. In particular, these methods work to increase (1) the number of dimensions that can be represented on plane surfaces and (2) the data density (amount of information per unit area).

IN this Japanese travel guide, an engaging hybrid of design technique, the abrupt shift from friendly perspective to hard flatland shows the loss suffered by giving in to the arbitrary data-compression of paper surfaces. A bird's-eye view with detailed perspective describes local areas near the architecturally renowned Ise Shrine; then, on the right margin, a very flat map delineates the national railroad system linking the shrine to major cities, somewhat compensating for loss of a visual dimension with a broad overview. A change in design accommodates a change in the scale of the map, and local detail is shown in national context, a mixed landscape of refuge and overview. The horizontal layout combines harmoniously with the vertical orientation of the language, so that the stand-up labels point precisely to each location.

Guide for Visitors to Ise Shrine (Ise, Japan; no date; published between October 1948 and April 1954, according to The Library, Ise Shrine, Mie Prefecture).

Mary C. Dickerson, *The Frog Book: North American Toads and Frogs, with a Study of the Habits and Life Histories of those of the Northeastern States* (New York, 1906), 74-75.

[2] John White, *The Birth and Rebirth of Pictorial Space* (London, 1957); and Lawrence Wright, *Perspective in Perspective* (London, 1983). See also the remarkable book by Kim Veltman, *Linear Perspective and the Visual Dimensions of Science and Art: Studies on Leonardo da Vinci I* (München, 1986).

[3] Redrawn from Emil v. Zmaczynski, "Periodic System of the Elements in a New Form," *Journal of Chemical Education*, 12 (1935), 265-267; Frank Austin Gooch and Claude Frederic Walker, *Outline of Inorganic Chemistry, II* (London, 1905), 8-9; and Andreas von Antropoff, "Eine neue Form des periodischen Systems der Elemente," *Zeitschrift für Angewandte Chemie*, 39 (1926), 722-728; Edward Mazurs, *Types of Graphic Representation of the Periodic System of Chemical Elements* (La Grange, Illinois, 1957).

When the toad (*Bufo americanus Le Conte*) sheds its skin upon the occasion of a quarterly moulting, the suit leaves life's spaceland and collapses into flatland, not unlike our information displays.

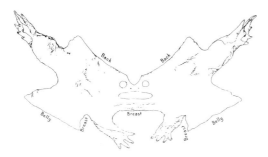

All sorts of techniques for doing better than flattened-out toad suits have evolved during some 500 years of information design.[2] Since the 15th-century Italian Renaissance, when Florentine architects perfected the necessary geometry, conventional perspective drawing has enriched representations of physical objects. And, for more abstract multivariate information not residing in our three-space reality, several enterprising methods have evolved—nearly silently, often to be found in workaday diagrams of those confronted with an overwhelming quantity of data. A few such techniques are well documented; for example, the elaborate structuring of the periodic table of chemical elements[3] (with several

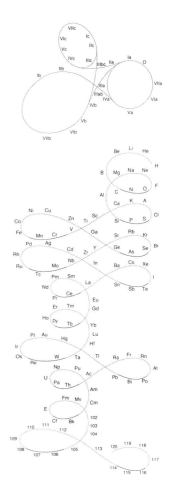

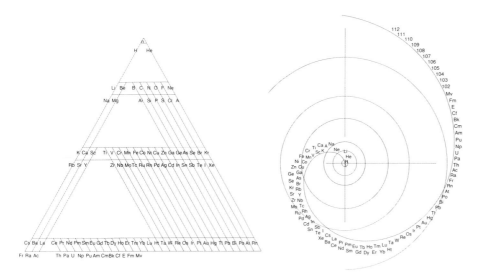

hundred arrangements proposed to capture the assorted complexities). Some recently perfected statistical graphics, self-consciously multivariate, enrich flatland with the dynamics of rotating point clouds on

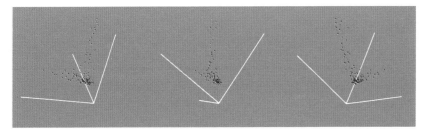

computer screens—a marvel, although navigation in three-dimensional scatterplots is not a trivial matter.[4] Another approach, here on the right, slices and projects data from many angles onto six of the twelve surfaces of a pentagonal dodecahedron (only six faces are needed, since opposite parallel faces show identical views).

Nearly every escape from flatland demands extensive compromise, trading off one virtue against another; the literature consists of partial, arbitrary, and particularistic solutions; and neither clever idiosyncratic nor conventionally adopted designs solve the inherent general difficulties of dimensional compression. Even our language, like our paper, often lacks immediate capacity to communicate a sense of dimensional complexity. Paul Klee wrote to this point:

> It is not easy to arrive at a conception of a whole which is constructed from parts belonging to different dimensions. And not only nature, but also art, her transformed image, is such a whole.

> It is difficult enough, oneself, to survey this whole, whether nature or art, but still more difficult to help another to such a comprehensive view.

> This is due to the consecutive nature of the only methods available to us for conveying a clear three-dimensional concept of an image in space, and results from deficiencies of a temporal nature in the spoken word.

> For, with such a medium of expression, we lack the means of discussing in its constituent parts, an image which possesses simultaneously a number of dimensions.[5]

And perspective projection is a simple extension of a two-surface, made unmistakable by everyday experience in three-space itself. Yet much of our data—and nature's pattern—have far greater complexity. What, then, are general strategies for extending the dimensional and informational reach of display flatlands? And what specific techniques effectively document and envision multivariate worlds? Why are some performances better than others?

To begin, a series of splendid examples.

[4] Andrew W. Donoho, David L. Donoho, Miriam Gasko, MACSPIN *Graphical Data Analysis Software* (Austin, Texas, 1985), illustration at p. 35 (redrawn); and the important 1974 paper by Mary Anne Fisherkeller, Jerome H. Friedman, and John W. Tukey, "PRIM-9: An Interactive Multidimensional Data Display and Analysis System," in William S. Cleveland, ed., *The Collected Works of John W. Tukey, Volume V, Graphics: 1965-1985* (Pacific Grove, California, 1988), 308-327. For a report of some difficulties, see Peter J. Huber, "Experiences with Three-Dimensional Scatterplots," *Journal of the American Statistical Association*, 82 (June 1987), 448-453.

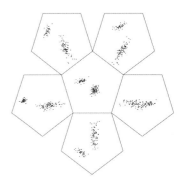

Showing the oft-plotted Anderson data for *Iris setosa* •, *Iris versicolor* •, and *Iris virginica* •, redrawn from Paul A. Tukey and John W. Tukey, "Preparation; Prechosen Sequences of Views," in V. Barnett, ed., *Interpreting Multivariate Data* (New York, 1981), 205-206.

[5] Paul Klee, *On Modern Art* (London, 1948), 15, translated by Paul Findlay from *Über die moderne Kunst* (Bern, 1945). Recent computer adventures seek to give dimensionality and nonlinearity to text. See E. J. Conklin, "Hypertext: An Introduction and Survey," *Computer* (September 1987), 17-41.

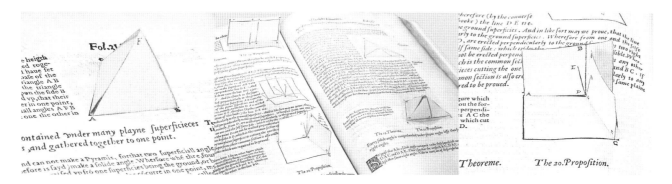

DIRECT methods for display of three dimensions include making models, as in this 1570 edition of Euclid's *Elements*, where little paper constructions teach solid geometry. Models pleasingly represent the smooth surfaces of three-space, as in architectural miniatures and curvaceous mathematical solids. More obstreperous statistical data, however, require models that fit noisy multivariate point clouds.

Narratives of the universe were impressively cranked up in orreries, simulations of our solar system (as known in 1800), with planets and their satellites rotating and orbiting. Although a triumph of gear ratios, the machines did commit a grave sin of information design—Pridefully Obvious Presentation—by directing attention more toward miraculous contraptionary display than to planetary motion.

Euclid, *The Elements of Geometrie* (London, 1570), with preface by John Dee, English translation by Henry Billingsley, fol. 314, 333. A fine guide to various extra-dimensional elaborations in book design is Gay Walker, *Eccentric Books* (New Haven: Yale University Library, 1988).

William Pearson, "Planetary Machines," in Abraham Rees, ed., *The Cyclopaedia; or, Universal Dictionary of Arts, Sciences, and Literature, Plates, Vol. IV* (London, 1820), plate XI; and Henry C. King with John R. Millburn, *Geared to the Stars: The Evolution of Planetariums, Orreries, and Astronomical Clocks* (Toronto, 1978).

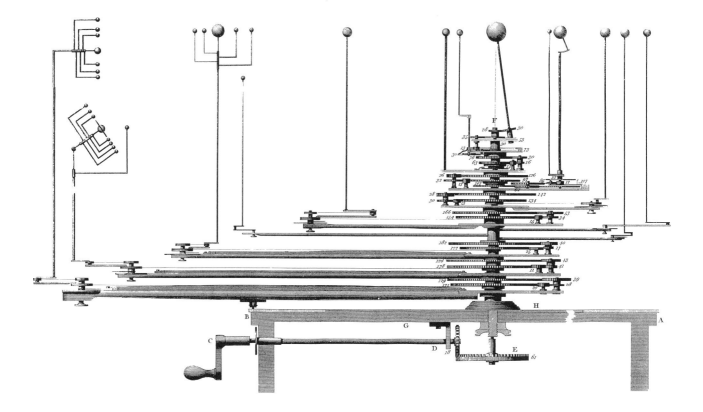

Color stereopair of Bonaduz, Canton of Grisons, Switzerland, October, 1975, photographs taken with Wild Leitz aerial camera RC10. Scale about 1:11,000.

[6] Stereoscopic viewers will assist in obtaining three-dimensional images. The effects can be seen without optical devices by some, however. The views here are arranged for the *wide-eyed* or *pie-eyed* method of viewing stereograms; those using the popular *cross-eyed* method will see sunken mountains and raised rivers. See Thomas Avery and Graydon Berlin, *Interpretation of Aerial Photographs* (Minneapolis, 4th edition, 1985), 25–90.

Particularly intriguing are stereo illustrations, which deliver vivid three-dimensional scenes by means of paired images (one for each eye), which are then fused mentally by viewers. Aerial landscapes, molecular structures, and other worldly objects are commonly portrayed; representations of more abstract and ragged quantitative data are rarely seen. Many viewers must struggle (and some fail) to fuse the images; even experienced eyes may require several minutes of vacant staring before obtaining the splendid stereo view.[6] Recent work on computer visualizations, stereo images, holograms, and so on hint at an increasing depth and pace to analytic displays, perhaps eventually without all the paraphernalia accompanying current methods.[7]

[7] Promising results are D. B. Carr, W. L. Nicholson, R. J. Littlefield, and D. L. Hall, "Interactive Color Display Methods for Multivariate Data," and K. R. Gabriel and C. L. Odoroff, "Illustrations of Model Diagnosis by Means of Three-Dimensional Biplots," in Edward J. Wegman and Douglas J. DePriest, *Statistical Image Processing and Graphics* (New York, 1986), 215–250, 258–274; Thomas V. Papathomas, James A. Schiavone, and Bela Julesz, "Stereo Animation for Very Large Data Bases," *Computer Graphics and Applications* (September, 1987), 18–27; and William S. Cleveland and Marylyn E. McGill, eds., *Dynamic Graphics for Statistics* (Belmont, California, 1988).

SUNSPOTS were examined in detail by telescope in the early 1600s, after some 200 years of repeated viewing by unaided eyes in Athens, China, Japan, and Russia. It was difficult for Europeans to see sunspots at all because Aristotle had said that celestial bodies were perfect and without blemish, a fancy which became official church doctrine in the middle ages.[8] Then, in 1610-1612, Galileo and others made detailed telescopic observations of sunspots.

Galileo marked spots directly onto paper flatland, maintaining the proper image plane while drawing a large diagram of a spotted sun:

> The method is this: Direct the telescope upon the sun as if you were going to observe that body. Having focused and steadied it, expose a flat white sheet of paper about a foot from the concave lens; upon this will fall a circular image of the sun's disk, with all spots that are on it arranged with exactly the same symmetry as in the sun. The more the paper is moved away from the tube, the larger this image will become, and the better the spots will be depicted. Thus they will all be seen without damage to the eye, even the smallest of them— which, when observed through the telescope, can scarcely be perceived, and only with fatigue and injury to the eyes.

[8] George Sarton, "Early Observations of the Sunspots," *Isis*, 37 (May 1947), 69-71; for the full history, D. Justin Schove, ed., *Sunspot Cycles* (Stroudsberg, Pennsylvania, 1983).

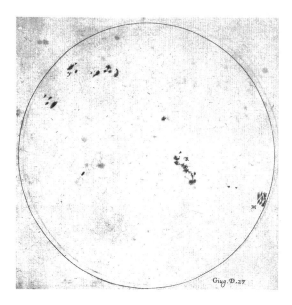

In order to picture them accurately, I first describe on the paper a circle of the size that best suits me, and then by moving the paper towards or away from the tube I find the exact place where the image of the sun is enlarged to the measure of the circle I have drawn. This also serves me as a norm and rule for getting the plane of the paper right, so that it will not be tilted to the luminous cone of sunlight that emerges from the telescope. For if the paper is oblique, the section will be oval and not circular, and therefore will not perfectly fit the circumference drawn on the paper. By tilting the paper the proper position is easily found, and then with a pen one may mark out spots in their right sizes, shapes, and positions. But one must work dextrously, following the movement of the sun and frequently moving the telescope, which must be kept directly on the sun.[9]

[9] Galileo Galilei, *History and Demonstrations Concerning Sunspots and Their Phenomena* (Rome, 1613), translated by Stillman Drake, *Discoveries and Opinions of Galileo* (Garden City, New York, 1957), 115-116.

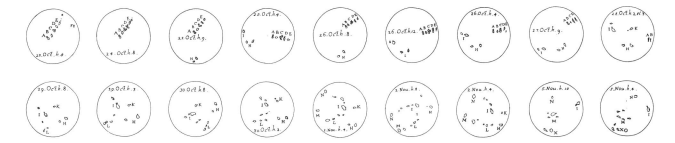

As more observations were collected daily, small multiple diagrams recorded the data indexed on time (a design simultaneously enhancing dimensionality and information density), with the labeled sunspots parading along alphabetically. This profoundly multivariate analysis—showing sunspot location in two-space, time, labels, and shifting relative orientation of the sun in our sky—reflects data complexities that arise because a rotating sun is observed from a rotating and orbiting earth:

Illustrations from Christopher Scheiner (writing under the pseudonym "Apelles"), *De Maculis Solaribus* (Rome, 1613), 14-15; and his *Rosa Ursina sive Sol* (Bracciani, 1626-1630), 63. On the dispute between Galileo and Scheiner concerning sunspots, see William Shea, *Galileo's Intellectual Revolution* (New York, 1972), 48-74.

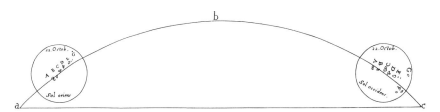

a c, horizon, a b c, arcus folis diurnus. Soloriens ex parte a, maculas exhibet quas vides, occidens verò c, easdem ratione primi motus, nonnihil inuertit. Et hanc matutinam vespertinamq̃ mutationem, omnes maculæ quotidie fubeunt. Quod femel exhibuiffe et monuiffe, fufficiat

For some astronomers, particularly those seeking to reconcile data with doctrine, it was unclear just where sunspots were located. Surely not on the surface of that perfect sphere; perhaps satellites orbited the sun, or even planets were in transit across the sun's face—speculations soon demolished by Galileo. Through an elegant chain of visual reasoning and with characteristic sardonic bluntness, Galileo, writing from Florence in August 1612, converts empirical observation into focused evidence supporting conclusions. His argument unfolds the raw data ("what the eye of the forehead" registers) into a luminous explanation of mechanism ("what the eye of the mind" envisions),[10] a deeply visual logic that produced precise insights far beyond those achieved by others who had also observed sunspots in the early 1600s. Indeed, "it was more than 150 years before any important addition was made"[11] to Galileo's results, as reported in 1613:

> I therefore repeat and more positively confirm to Your Excellency that the dark spots seen in the solar disk by means of the telescope are not at all distant from its surface, but are either contiguous to it or separated by an interval so small as to be quite imperceptible. Nor are they stars or other permanent bodies, but some are

[10] The persistent relationship between artistic capacity for visualization and extraordinary scientific achievement is described in Robert Scott Root-Bernstein, "Visual Thinking: The Art of Imagining Reality," *Transactions of the American Philosophical Society*, 75 (1985), 50-67. For further evidence about Galileo, see Erwin Panofsky, *Galileo as a Critic of the Arts* (The Hague, 1954), 5: "An excellent draughtsman, Galileo loved and understood 'with perfect taste' all the 'arts subordinated to design' . . . he was originally inclined to study painting rather than mathematics, and one of his most intimate and faithful friends was the outstanding painter of their native Florence, Ludovico Cigoli."

[11] R. J. Bray and R. E. Loughhead, *Sunspots* (London, 1964), 2. Galileo's analysis attained special longevity because of its insight and also the nearly complete absence of observable sunspots from 1645 until 1715! John A. Eddy, "The Maunder Minimum," *Science*, 192 (June 18, 1976), 1189-1202.

always being produced and others dissolved. They vary in duration from one or two days to thirty or forty. For the most part they are of most irregular shape, and their shapes continually change, some quickly and violently, others more slowly and moderately.

They also vary in darkness, appearing sometimes to condense and sometimes to spread out and rarefy. In addition to changing shape, some of them divide into three or four, and often several unite into one; this happens less at the edge of the sun's disk than in its central parts. Besides all these disordered movements they have in common a general uniform motion across the face of the sun in parallel lines. From special characteristics of this motion one may learn that the sun is absolutely spherical, that it rotates from west to east around its own center, carries the spots along with it in parallel circles, and completes an entire revolution in about one lunar month. Also worth noting is the fact that the spots always fall in one zone of the solar body, lying between the two circles which bound the declinations of the planets—that is, they fall within 28° or 29° of the sun's equator.

The different densities and degrees of darkness of the spots, their changes of shape, and their collecting and separating are evident directly to our sight, without any need of reasoning, as a glance at the diagrams which I am enclosing will show. But that the spots are contiguous to the sun and are carried around by its rotation can only be deduced and concluded by reasoning from certain particular events which our observations yield.

First, to see twenty or thirty spots at a time move with one common movement is a strong reason for believing that each does not go wandering about by itself, in the manner of the planets going around the sun. . . . To begin with, the spots at their first appearance and final disappearance near the edges of the sun generally seem to have very little breadth, but to have the same length that they show in the central parts of the sun's disk. Those who understand what is meant by foreshortening on a spherical surface will see this to be a manifest argument that the sun is a globe, that the spots are close to its surface, and that as they are carried on that surface toward the center they will always grow in breadth while preserving the same length. . . . this maximum thinning, it is clear, takes place at the point of greatest foreshortening. . . .

I have since been much impressed by the courtesy of nature, which thousands of years ago arranged a means by which we might come to notice these spots, and through them to discover things of greater consequence. For without any instruments, from any little hole through which sunlight passes, there emerges an image of the sun with its spots, and at a distance this becomes stamped upon any surface opposite the hole. It is true that these spots are not nearly as sharp as those seen through the telescope, but the majority of them may nevertheless be seen. If in church some day Your Excellency sees the light of the sun falling upon the pavement at a distance from some broken window pane, you may catch this light upon a flat white sheet of paper, and there you will perceive the spots. I might add that nature has been so kind that for our instruction she has sometimes marked the sun with a spot so large and dark as to be seen merely by the naked eye, though the false and inveterate idea that the heavenly bodies are devoid of all mutation or alteration has made people believe that such a spot was the planet Mercury coming between us and the sun, to the disgrace of past astronomers.[12]

[12] Galileo Galilei, *History and Demonstrations Concerning Sunspots and Their Phenomena* (Rome, 1613), translated by Stillman Drake, *Discoveries and Opinions of Galileo* (Garden City, New York, 1957), 106-107, 116-117. Galileo had been through all this once before when he first saw craters on the moon, another supposedly perfect celestial sphere. One of Galileo's opponents, "who admitted the surface of the moon looked rugged, maintained that it was actually quite smooth and spherical as Aristotle had said, reconciling the two ideas by saying that the moon was covered with a smooth transparent material through which mountains and craters inside it could be discerned. Galileo, sarcastically applauding the ingenuity of this contribution, offered to accept it gladly—provided that his opponent would do him the equal courtesy of allowing him then to assert that the moon was even more rugged than he had thought before, its surface being covered with mountains and craters of this invisible substance ten times as high as any he had seen. At Pisa the leading philosopher had refused even to look through the telescope; when he died a few months afterward, Galileo expressed the hope that since he had neglected to look at the new celestial objects while on earth, he would now see them on his way to heaven." Stillman Drake, "Introduction: Second Part," *Discoveries and Opinions of Galileo* (Garden City, New York, 1957), 73.

With continuing observation, indexing each image afresh grew cumbersome. Christopher Scheiner's *Rosa Ursina sive Sol*, completed in 1630, arrays the apparent path of spots across a stationary disk,

Christopher Scheiner, *Rosa Ursina sive Sol* (Bracciani, 1626-1630), 317, 325, 333, and 339.

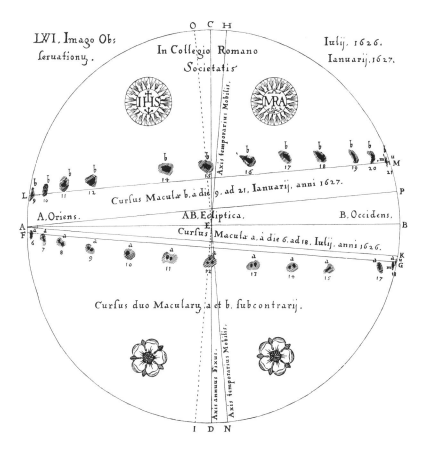

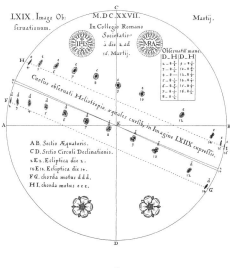

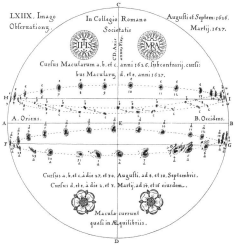

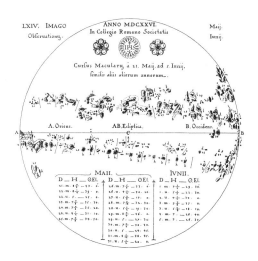

an ingenious method for tracking simple sunspot structures but tending to jumble up complex data. Symbols of Scheiner's patron and religious order decorate those areas without spots in a hundred such diagrams, a reminder of Jonathan Swift's indictment of 17th-century cartographers who substituted embellishment for data:

> With savage pictures fill their gaps,
> And o'er unhabitable downs,
> Place elephants for want of towns

These symbols, similar to a modern trademark or logotype, may have served as a seal of validation for the readers of 1630. Today they appear somewhat strident, contradicting nature's rich pattern.

Years and years of daily mapping led to this superb visualization, sunspot distribution in latitude, recorded for long time periods. The sunspot's two areal dimensions are reduced to one content-relevant dimension, as the immense quantity of data provoked design mastery. E. W. Maunder's 1904 butterfly diagram aggregates the micro-detail of individual observations into a macro-view, portraying a *distributional* cycle of sunspots moving from the center of each hemisphere toward the equator, as Galileo had noted.[13] Only an interval ±40° sun latitude is plotted, for little activity is seen in more extreme latitudes:

[13] E.W. Maunder, "Notes on the Distribution of Sun-Spots in Heliographic Latitude, 1874 to 1902," *Royal Astronomical Society Monthly Notices*, 64 (1904), 747-761. The data compression here consists of taking only the *vertical* dimension of the sunspot, measured in degrees latitude.

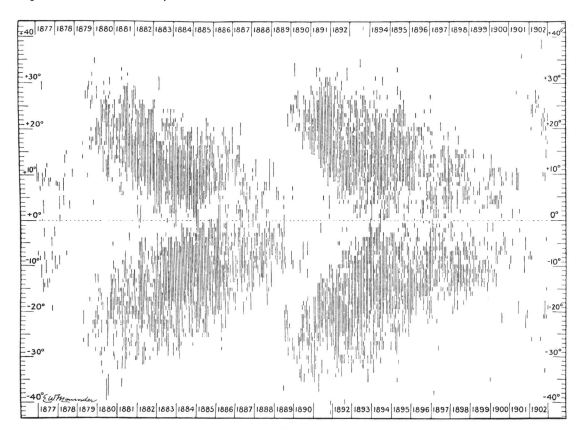

The fine detail of this sunspot diagram merges into a repeated typical pattern; and, as the data march along over time, the foremost result is a visual measure of *variation* around that average. Measured assessments of variability are at the heart of quantitative reasoning. R. A. Fisher, the founder of modern statistics, wrote in 1925:

> The populations which are the object of statistical study always display variation in one or more respects. To speak of statistics as the study of variation also serves to emphasize the contrast between the aims of modern statisticians and those of their predecessors. For until comparatively recent times, the vast majority of workers in this field appear to have had no other aim than to ascertain aggregate, or average, values. The variation itself was not an object of study, but was recognized rather as a troublesome circumstance which detracted from the value of the average. The

error curve of the *mean* of a normal sample has been familiar for a century, but that of the *standard deviation* was the object of researches up to 1915. Yet, from the modern point of view, the study of the causes of variation of any variable phenomenon, from the yield of wheat to the intellect of [people], should be begun by the examination and measurement of the variation which presents itself.[14]

[14] Ronald A. Fisher, *Statistical Methods for Research Workers* (Edinburgh, 1925; 13th edition, 1958), 3.

Compared to Maunder's original picture, the modern butterfly diagram increases the data density tenfold, reporting now a full century of solar memoirs. And, moving in parallel with the flapping wings, the lower time-series restores an areal measure of sunspot activity.[15] The display method used here, parallel sequencing, enhances dimensionality and density, although showing the variables one-at-a-time-in-parallel is unrevealing of complex *interrelated* structure. (As statisticians explain, marginal distributions are not wholly informative with regard to joint distributions.) Portrayal of nine full cycles here enforces comfortable comparisons of between- and within-cycle variation, and also exposes an apparent growth trend (perhaps it is merely improved observation) in the wingspan of recent cycles.

[15] Since the sunspots appear symmetric about the sun's equator, the wings may be folded over to show the distribution of the sun latitude of spots without distinction between northerly and southerly sunspots. W. Gleissberg and T. Damboldt, "A New Approach to the Butterfly Diagram of Sunspots," *Journal of the British Astronomical Association*, 81 (1971), 271–276.

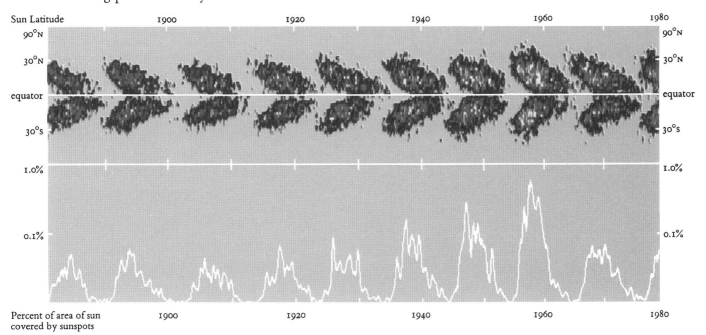

Sun Latitude

90°N · 30°N · equator · 30°S · 1.0% · 0.1%

90°N · 30°N · equator · 30°S · 1.0% · 0.1%

1900 · 1920 · 1940 · 1960 · 1980

Percent of area of sun covered by sunspots

1900 · 1920 · 1940 · 1960 · 1980

Note all the different techniques for displaying sunspots during 380 years of data analysis—from Galileo's first precious observation of the solar disk, to small multiple images, to dimensionality and data compression, and finally to micro/macro displays combining pattern and detail, average and variation. *Exactly the same design strategies are found, again and again, in the work of those faced with a flood of data and images, as they scramble to reveal, within the cramped limits of flatland, their detailed and complex information. These design strategies are surprisingly widespread, albeit little appreciated, and occur quite independently of the content of the data.*

At top, a Maunder diagram from 1880 to 1980, with the sine of the latitude marking sunspot placement. Color coding (the lighter, the larger) reflects the logarithm of the area covered by sunspots within each areal bin of data. The lower time-series, by summing over all latitudes, shows the total area of the sun's surface covered by sunspots at any given time during the hundred-year sequence. Diagrams produced by David H. Hathaway, George C. Marshall Space Flight Center, National Aeronautics and Space Administration.

WONDROUSLY complex is this graphic timetable for a Java railroad line, Soerabaja-Djokjakarta, drawn in November 1937 (annotated in Dutch, then in Japanese). By smoothly suppressing a dimension first here and then several times there, finessing perspective treatments entirely, and changing the focus, this 24-hour railroad plan abstractly traces out multiple paths through three-space and time, in a four-dimensional tour with a dozen other variables carried along.

The time scale is read across the top; towns on the railroad route are indicated by names stacked down the column at left. Diagonal lines running from upper left to lower right show trains heading down \\, return trains by diagonals going from lower left to upper right //. The first train from the top station, Soerabajakotta, leaves at about 4:50 in the morning (at the • dot), and then reaches the first stop just a few minutes later, and so on. Steeper lines are the faster trains. When trains going opposite directions pass by, an X appears. The arrangement repays meticulous study:

• Graphical timetables turn the three spatial dimensions of our daily world into one train-relevant dimension by measuring distance along the track itself. Horizontal grid lines, marking towns and station stops, are spaced approximately in proportion to their distance apart along the rails (yielding straight-line diagonals, assuming trains run more or less at constant speed over the entire route).

• The left margin of the timetable reflects another viewpoint, with a profile (at an enlarged vertical scale) of all the valleys and mountains crossed by rail. This visual depiction is accompanied by quantitative details, to the right of the profile, where columns of numbers describe the grade and path. Note how the vertical has been used repeatedly to

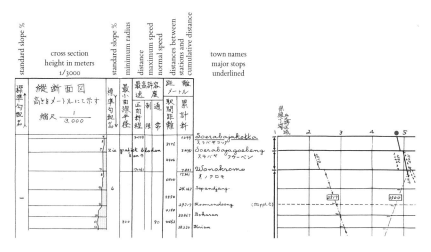

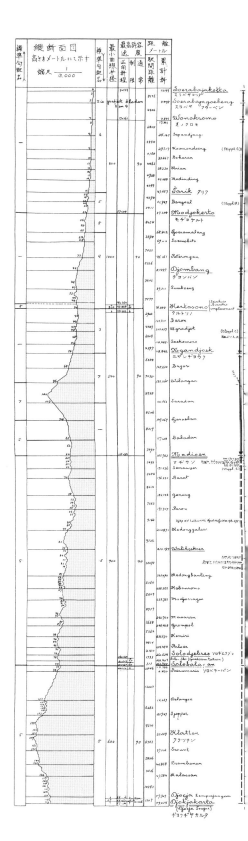

array parallel sequences of thoroughgoing data. In flatland, after all, every opportunity to spread additional information over an already available dimension must be cherished.

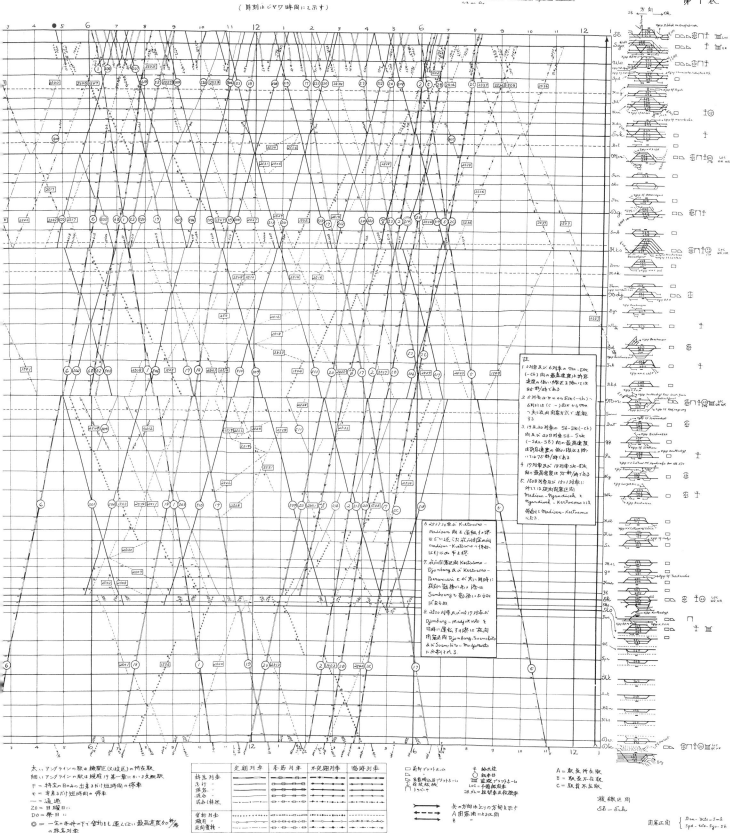

• Within each station, still another view—for what is important here is activity on the flat ground. Aerial views of the intricate networks of station switching tracks are shown, encoded with symbols, icons, and dingbats describing the local facilities:

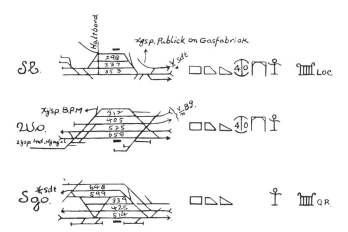

□ ▷	cargo unloading platform
▷	livestock loading platform
④⓪ ⊓	cargo unloading facilities
⚲	water supply pump tower
⑫	directional change platform
▥	car repair platform
Loc	standby engines
QR	relief car
Spd	closed areas

• The train diagonals cleverly multiple-function,[16] as those marks record six variables all at once: the location of a train between towns, time of that position, direction, train type, relative speed (comparing slopes of diagonals), and yearly pattern of operation. A two-dimensional matrix organizes lines by type and seasonality, encoding the diagonal path of the train through the space-time field:

[16] The idea of double-functioning elements appears in architectural criticism; Robert Venturi, *Complexity and Contradiction in Architecture* (New York, 2nd edition, 1977), ch. 5. Venturi in turn cites Wylie Sypher, *Four Stages of Renaissance Style* (Garden City, New York, 1955). For statistical graphics, see "Multifunctioning Graphical Elements," in Edward R. Tufte, *The Visual Display of Quantitative Information* (Cheshire, Connecticut, 1983), 139-159.

		regular	seasonal	irregular	special
		定期列車	季節列車	不定期列車	臨時列車
super express	特急列車				
express	急行 〃				
passenger	旅客 〃				
mixed	混合 〃				
special	〃（特殊）				
cargo	貨物列車				
preferential	職用 〃				
night cargo	夜間貨物 〃				

This 16-variable schedule served as an internal planning document for the Java Railroad; it was then obtained by agents working for Japan preparing for their military invasion of Java during 1942.[17] In the upper righthand corner, this railroad timetable is classified "secret" (祕). The spy graphical timetable portrays detailed operations of an intricate and irregular system and, at a more distant view, the overall structure and pattern of the railroad—a dual micro and macro reading. It is very much like an excellent map, but with many dimensions breaking free of direct analogy to conventional cartographic flatland.

[17] *Indonesia ni okeru nihon gunsei no genkyu* [*A Study of Japanese Occupation in Indonesia*], Okuma Social Science Center at Waseda University (Tokyo, 1959).

Kellom Tomlinson, *The Art of Dancing, Explained by Reading and Figures* (London, 1735), book I, plate XII.

[18] Ann Hutchinson Guest, *Dance Notation: The Process of Recording Movement on Paper* (London, 1984), 14. This book also makes a surprising demonstration that abstract, symbolic methods of movement notation are preferable to film and stick figure portrayals, at least from a dancer's viewpoint.

LIKE the tour-guides for the Ise Shrine and sunspots, movements are again depicted on a perspective map, but now in four dimensions—the flatland of floor, coded gestures in dance notation of body motion, and time sequence. (Symbolically encoded because "any serious system of movement notation avoids words because they are a strong deterrent to international communication."[18]) The floor plan is linked to the airy music (two dimensions there, time and tone) by numbers, with varying steps for varying sounds. The numbers double-function, simultaneously sequencing steps and relating movement to music. Note the enlarged dance-floor notation for the partner on our right, since he takes a front route in switching sides. Often the redundancy of bilateral symmetry consumes space better devoted to fresh information; but here the integrated complexity of dual movements, as the dancers' paths weave and intermingle, requires symmetric repetition. The two, pulled apart by their mirrored pairing, become visually integrated through their nearly touching hands, mutual postures, overlapping paths of movement, and convergence of perspective lines radiating from the flatland floor to a vanishing point exactly midway between their outstretched hands. A subtle, graceful, profoundly simple design, with a straightforward complexity, a forerunner of modern dance and movement notation.

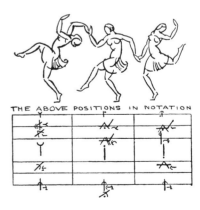

Margaret Morris, *The Notation of Movement* (London, 1928), 103-104.

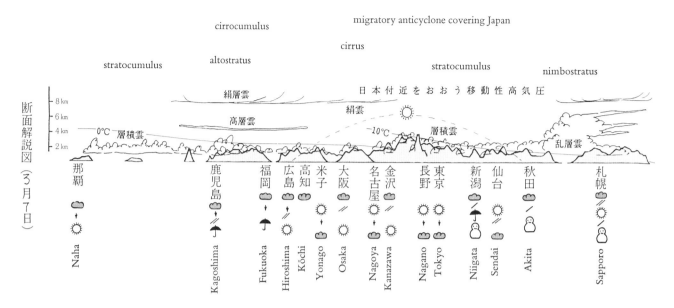

cirrocumulus

migratory anticyclone covering Japan

cirrus

stratocumulus   altostratus   stratocumulus   nimbostratus

断面解説図（3月7日）

8 km   6 km   4 km   2 km

絹層雲   日本付近をおおう移動性高気圧

高層雲   絹雲

0°C   層積雲   -10°C   層積雲   乱層雲

那覇   鹿児島   福岡   広島   高知   米子   大阪   名古屋   金沢   長野   東京   新潟   仙台   秋田   札幌

Naha   Kagoshima   Fukuoka   Hiroshima   Kōchi   Yonago   Osaka   Nagoya   Kanazawa   Nagano   Tokyo   Niigata   Sendai   Akita   Sapporo

HERE gray contours tracing out constant temperatures at 0° and -10°C stretch through the clouds in a side profile of Japan, an ocean-eye view. Forecasts for 15 areas annotate the cross-section of this unusual weather map from a daily newspaper. How easily the design reads, compared to traditional weather maps that commit both their visual dimensions to a planview of latitude and longitude, suppressing the vertical. Of course the arrangement works best for long, thin countries.

The next graphic, plotted by a computer, reports four times daily the levels of three air pollutants fuming over southern California. Nitrogen oxides (top row) are emitted by power plants, refineries, and vehicles. Refineries along the coast produce post-midnight peaks shown in the first panel; cars and power plants send daytime levels up. The morning traffic generates carbon monoxide, with high concentrations where five freeways converge in downtown Los Angeles. Reactive hydrocarbons (bottom row) emanate from refineries after midnight and then increase

Redrawn from *Akahata* [Red Flag], Tokyo, March 7, 1985. English translation added here. Note the changing weather reported for some cities, for example, Sapporo at the far right of the map.

Redrawn. See G. J. McRae, W. R. Goodin, and J. H. Seinfeld, "Development of a Second-Generation Mathematical Model for Urban Air Pollution. I. Model Formulation," *Atmospheric Environment*, 16 (1982), 679-696.

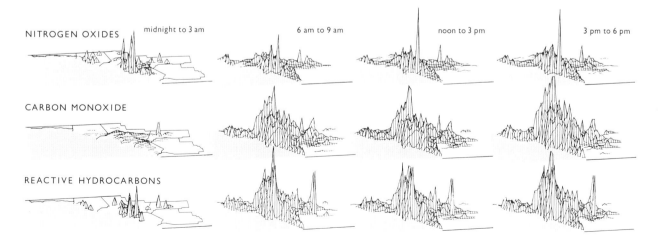

NITROGEN OXIDES   midnight to 3 am   6 am to 9 am   noon to 3 pm   3 pm to 6 pm

CARBON MONOXIDE

REACTIVE HYDROCARBONS

with daily traffic. The twelve time-space-pollutant maps add up smog observations on a spatial grid of 2,400 squares (each five kilometers on a side), for a total of 28,800 readings, except for those masked by peaks—a high density arrangement of data, abounding with variables and with observations on those variables.

This air pollution display is a *small multiple*, with the same design structure repeated for all the images. An economy of perception results; once viewers decode and comprehend the design for one slice of data, they have familiar access to data in all the other slices. As our eye moves from one image to the next, this constancy of design allows viewers to focus on changes in information rather than changes in graphical composition. A steady canvas makes for a clearer picture. Note how paper's two dimensions are put to work here, twice over. Each small map reports on the two-space location of a third quantity; those maps become entries themselves in another matrix arraying time of day by type of pollution, for a grand total of five variables.

Tabular arrays of numbers similarly confront flatland, with design solutions identical to graphical displays. These compound interest tables record a third variable located on the two-surface, and then repeat each array, small multiple style, at levels of a fourth variable. Entries show capital plus interest, entabled for sequenced amounts of capital and time. That grid is then repeated, indexed on the annual rate of interest.

Data entries located on a plane surface can themselves multiply, as in the notorious applicant/admit tables for law school admissions. Knitting together all combinations of college grades and test scores, the bivariate grid registers both the number of applicants and, from those candidates, the number then actually admitted by this law school. The margins on the right and bottom sum up to univariate distributions, with grand totals shown at lower right. This table could in turn become an entry in another two-space, a multiple comparison over time of various schools. And when that array itself becomes another entry . . .

LAW SCHOOL APTITUDE TEST (LSAT) PERCENTILE

GPA	0-30	31-40	41-50	51-60	61-70	71-80	81-90	91-99	TOTALS
>3.75	7-0	7-0	13-3	18-0	34-1	71-9	151-36	449-345	750-394
3.75	21-1	26-4	38-6	54-0	94-0	206-14	358-19	791-436	1588-480
3.50	57-4	37-4	53-5	65-2	136-5	228-8	369-6	798-148	1743-182
3.25	88-0	59-5	61-0	96-5	131-8	193-7	289-12	504-44	1421-81
3.00	93-0	46-0	46-0	53-0	79-1	89-3	122-2	204-7	732-13
<2.75	174-0	55-0	44-0	51-0	53-0	74-0	80-0	113-2	644-2
TOTALS	440-5	230-13	255-14	337-7	527-15	861-41	1369-75	2859-982	6878-1152

INTÉRÊTS COMPOSÉS A TROIS POUR CENT.

CAPITAL.	1.re ANNÉE.		2.e ANNÉE.		3.e ANNÉE.	
f.	f.	e.	f.	e.	f.	e.
1	1	03	1	06	1	09
2	2	06	2	12	2	18
3	3	09	3	18	3	27
4	4	12	4	24	4	37
5	5	15	5	30	5	46
6	6	18	6	36	6	55
7	7	21	7	42	7	64
8	8	24	8	48	8	74
9	9	27	9	54	9	83
10	10	30	10	60	10	92
20	20	60	21	20	21	85
30	30	90	31	80	32	78
40	41	20	42	40	43	70
50	51	50	53	04	54	63
60	61	80	63	65	65	56
70	72	10	74	26	76	49
80	82	40	84	87	87	41
90	92	70	95	48	98	34
100	103	00	106	09	109	27
200	206	00	212	18	218	54
300	309	00	318	27	327	81
400	412	00	424	36	437	09
500	515	00	530	45	546	36
600	618	00	636	54	655	63
700	721	00	742	63	764	90
800	824	00	848	72	874	18
900	927	00	954	81	983	45
1,000	1,030	00	1,060	90	1,092	72
2,000	2,060	00	2,121	80	2,185	45
3,000	3,090	00	3,182	70	3,278	18

INTÉRÊTS COMPOSÉS A QUATRE POUR CENT.

CAPITAL.	1.re ANNÉE.		2.e ANNÉE.		3.e ANNÉE.	
f.	f.	e.	f.	e.	f.	e.
1	1	04	1	08	1	12
2	2	08	2	16	2	24
3	3	12	3	24	3	37
4	4	16	4	32	4	49
5	5	20	5	40	5	62
6	6	24	6	48	6	74
7	7	28	7	57	7	87
8	8	32	8	65	8	99
9	9	36	9	73	10	12
10	10	40	10	81	11	24
20	20	80	21	63	22	49
30	31	20	32	44	33	74
40	41	60	43	26	44	99
50	52	00	54	08	56	24
60	62	40	64	89	67	49
70	72	80	75	71	78	74
80	83	20	86	52	89	98
90	93	60	97	34	101	23
100	104	00	108	16	112	48
200	208	00	216	32	224	97
300	312	00	324	48	337	45
400	416	00	432	64	449	94
500	520	00	540	80	562	43
600	624	00	648	96	674	91
700	728	00	757	12	787	40
800	832	00	865	28	899	89
900	936	00	973	44	1,012	37
1,000	1,040	00	1,081	60	1,124	86
2,000	2,080	00	2,163	20	2,249	72
3,000	3,120	00	3,244	80	3,374	59

Barême Universel (Paris, 1822), 382-390.

Law School Admission Council and the Association of American Law Schools, *Pre-Law Handbook 1983-84.* (Washington, DC, 1983). The table shown is for the School of Law, New York University. Redrawn.

Small multiples work as efficient and convincing summaries of data or an argument, making the same point again and again by offering complementary variations on the major substantive theme. Here is the colorful story of one such chart:

The New York Times, March 14, 1987, 1.

GOTTI IS ACQUITTED BY A FEDERAL JURY IN CONSPIRACY CASE

NEW CHARGES ARE LIKELY

Verdict is the First Setback in Recent Government Drive Against Mafia Leaders

By LEONARD BUDER

John Gotti was acquitted of Federal racketeering and conspiracy charges yesterday in the Government's first major setback in its recent assault on organized crime.

Mr. Gotti, who the Government says is the leader of the nation's most powerful Mafia family, and six co-defendants were found not guilty of charges they took part in a criminal enterprise. They were accused of carrying out illegal gambling and loan-sharking operations, armed hijackings and at least two murders over an 18-year period.

Despite yesterday's verdict, Federal investigators said the 46-year-old Mr. Gotti might face indictment on new charges as head of the Gambino crime family. "I can't comment but I won't deny it," said Thomas L. Sheer, head of the Federal Bureau of Investigation in New York, when asked if the F.B.I. was building up another case against Mr. Gotti.

'We'll Be Starting Again'

"They'll be ready to frame us again in two weeks," Mr. Gotti told a reporter before leaving the Brooklyn courthouse in a gray Cadillac that was waiting for him. "In three weeks we'll be starting again, just watch."

Until yesterday, Federal prosecutors in the Southern and Eastern Districts of New York had recorded a string of successes in major organized-crime cases.

Within the last six months, the heads of the city's four other Mafia families have been convicted after trials in Manhattan and Brooklyn. They, like Mr. Gotti and his co-defendants, had been charged under the Federal Racketeer Influenced and Corrupt Organizations Act, or RICO.

Key Witnesses Were Criminals

"Obviously they perceived there was something wrong with the evidence," said Andrew J. Maloney, the United States Attorney in Brooklyn, referring to the jury.

Many of the Government's key witnesses were criminals who testified for the prosecution under grants of immunity or in return for payments and other benefits.

The last piece of evidence requested by the jury for re-examination was a chart introduced by the defense that showed the criminal backgrounds of seven prosecution witnesses. It listed 69 crimes, including murder, drug possession and sales and kidnapping.

Mr. Gotti's lawyer, Bruce Cutler, said the jury showed "courage" because "it's not easy to say no to a Federal prosecutor." He said the jury had not been impressed with the testimony of "paid Government informants who lie, who use drugs, who kill people."

The verdict, which came on the seventh day of jury deliberations after a trial that lasted almost seven months, surprised many in the packed courtroom. Friends of the defendants cheered and applauded; the Government prosecutors, Diane F. Giacalone and John Gleeson, looked glum.

Mr. Gotti, who has been dubbed "Dapper Don" because of his expensive attire and impeccable grooming, and his co-defendants hugged and kissed each other and their lawyers.

Then they stood and applauded as the 12 members of the jury — whose identities had been kept secret to prevent possible tampering — left the room escorted by Federal marshals....

The New York Times

John Gotti

A Weakness In Gotti Case

Major U.S. Witnesses Viewed as Unreliable

By SELWYN RAAB

Many lawyers and prosecutors who followed events in the seven-month trial of John Gotti said the underlying weakness of the prosecution's case was its apparent reliance on turncoat career criminals as key witnesses against Mr. Gotti and six co-defendants.

News Analysis

A signal that the credibility of the prosecution's principal witnesses was in doubt came yesterday morning when the jury, in its final request before acquitting the defendants of all charges, reviewed an exhibit introduced by the defense.

It was a chart listing the lengthy criminal records of seven prosecution witnesses who had obtained promises of leniency and other favors from the Government in return for their testimony against Mr. Gotti....

The chart invites reading both horizontally and vertically; neither direction enhances the reputations of those testifying against Mr. Gotti and his colleagues, as the eye detects curious patterns and unbroken runs of X's. Mr. Polisi, for example, has something of a streak going. Those marks indicating each crime by each witness are not modest or shy, and they dominate the spreadsheet grid (although only 37 percent of all the possible combinations are marked). Placement of particularly obnoxious activities at the top (murder) and bottom of the list (pistol whipping a priest) exploits the visual prominence of those positions.

United States v. Gotti, et al., 1987. Chart supplied by counsel, Bruce Cutler and Susan G. Kellman.

CRIMINAL ACTIVITY OF GOVERNMENT INFORMANTS

CRIME	CARDINALE	LOFARO	MALONEY	POLISI	SENATORE	FORONJY	CURRO
MURDER	X	X					
ATTEMPTED MURDER		X	X				
HEROIN POSSESSION AND SALE	X	X		X			X
COCAINE POSSESSION AND SALE	X		X	X			
MARIJUANA POSSESSION AND SALE							X
GAMBLING BUSINESS		X		X		X	
ARMED ROBBERIES	X		X	X	X		X
LOANSHARKING		X		X			
KIDNAPPING			X	X			
EXTORTION			X	X			
ASSAULT	X		X	X			X
POSSESSION OF DANGEROUS WEAPONS	X	X	X	X	X		X
PERJURY		X				X	
COUNTERFEITING					X	X	
BANK ROBBERY			X	X			
ARMED HIJACKING				X	X		
STOLEN FINANCIAL DOCUMENTS			X	X	X		
TAX EVASION				X		X	
BURGLARIES	X	X		X	X		
BRIBERY		X		X			
THEFT: AUTO, MONEY, OTHER			X	X	X	X	X
BAIL JUMPING AND ESCAPE			X	X			
INSURANCE FRAUDS					X	X	
FORGERIES				X	X		
PISTOL WHIPPING A PRIEST	X						
SEXUAL ASSAULT ON MINOR							X
RECKLESS ENDANGERMENT							X

Such displays are likely to be especially persuasive and memorable in situations where most information communicated consists of spoken words—as in a trial.[19] Courtroom graphics can overcome the linear, nonreversible, one-dimensional sequencing of talk talk talk, allowing members of a jury to reason about an array of data at their own pace and in their own manner. Visual displays of information encourage a diversity of individual viewer styles and rates of editing, personalizing, reasoning, and understanding. Unlike speech, visual displays are simultaneously a wideband and a perceiver-controllable channel.

[19] For visual displays in the courtroom, see Larry Gillen, ed., *Photographs and Maps Go to Court* (Washington, DC: American Society for Photogrammetry and Remote Sensing, 1986); and Gregory P. Joseph, *Modern Visual Evidence* (New York, 1989).

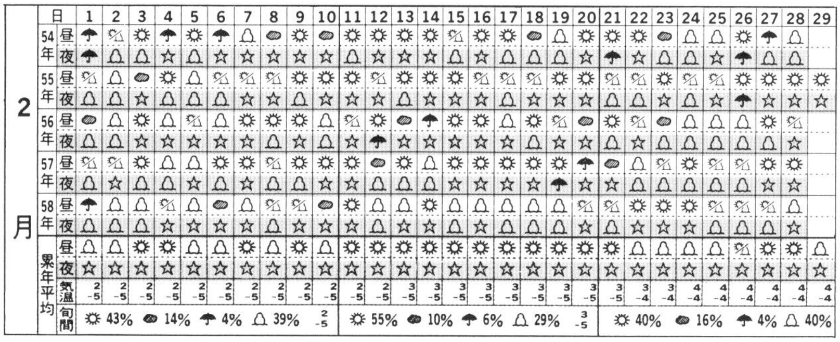

Legend (right of top chart):

☼ sunny day

☆ starry night

☁ cloudy

☂ rain

△ snow

This weather history above extends the technique, partitioning data by town, year, month, day, and day/night. Here are five years of daily and nightly Aomori weather every day in February. Bottom rows report summary data, averaged over ten-day periods, recounting the (1) most frequently observed weather, 1967–1982; (2) average high and low temperatures, last 30 years, 1951–1980; and (3) daytime frequency of sunshine, clouds, and rain during the last 16 years. A splendid total of 414 pieces of data are smoothly entabled, conveying both a sense of *average* and of *variation* about that average—the two fundamental summary measures of statistical data.

An even more concentrated history, below, of Tokyo climate divides a full decade of observations by town, year, month, and day. Especially adroit is the gathering of both dimensions of the paper to apportion the one-dimensional variable, time, into increments from fine to coarse; each year-by-day-matrix is compounded by months, stretching the range of a compact display into an abundant span of 1,826 days of weather history. High-information graphics, such as this, convey a spirit of quantitative depth and a sense of statistical integrity. Emaciated data-thin designs, in contrast, provoke suspicions—and rightfully so—about the quality of measurement and analysis.

Redrawn from *Weather Chart, 1984* (Tokyo, 1985), 42.

Redrawn from *Kisho Nenkan 1984* [*The 1984 Meteorological Almanac*], The Meteorology Agency and Japan Meteorology Association (Tokyo, 1984), 134–135.

○ Clear. Average amount of clouds less than 15% for all day (3:00, 9:00, 15:00, 21:00).

◑ Fair. Average amount of clouds more than 15% and less than 84% for all day.

◎ Cloudy. Average amount of clouds more than 85%.

• Light rain. Rain more than 1 mm but less than 5 mm.

● Rain. More than 5 mm in 24 hours.

* Snow. More than 1 cm during day.

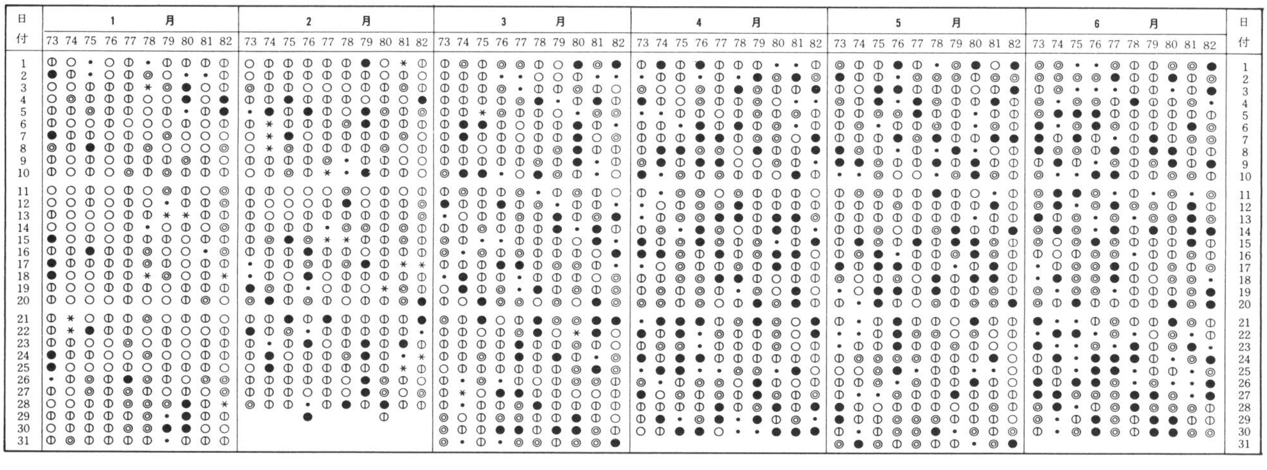

Small multiples, whether tabular or pictorial, move to the heart of visual reasoning—to see, distinguish, choose (even among children's shirts). Their multiplied smallness enforces local comparisons within our eyespan, relying on an active eye to select and make contrasts rather than on bygone memories of images scattered over pages and pages.

Redrawn from Yumi Takahashi and Ikuyo Shibukawa, *Color Coordination* (Tokyo, 1985), 114-115.

We envision information in order to reason about, communicate, document, and preserve that knowledge—activities nearly always carried out on two-dimensional paper and computer screen. Escaping this flatland and enriching the density of data displays are the essential tasks of information design. Such escapes grow more difficult as ties of data to our familiar three-space world weaken (with more abstract measures) and as the number of dimensions increases (with more complex data). Still, all the history of information displays and statistical graphics—indeed of any communication device—is entirely a progress of methods for enhancing density, complexity, dimensionality, and even sometimes beauty. Some of these methods, identified and described in the chapters that follow, include micro/macro readings of detail and panorama, layering and separation of data, multiplying of images, color, and narratives of space and time.

By giving the focus over to data rather than data-containers, these design strategies are transparent and self-effacing in character. Designs so good that they are invisible. Too many data presentations, alas, seek to attract and divert attention by means of display apparatus and ornament. Chartjunk has come to corrupt all sorts of information exhibits and computer interfaces, just like the "ducks" of modern architecture:

> When Modern architects righteously abandoned ornament on buildings, they unconsciously designed buildings that *were* ornament. In promoting Space and Articulation over symbolism and ornament, they distorted the whole building into a duck. They substituted for the innocent and inexpensive practice of applied

Big Duck, Flanders, New York; photograph by Edward Tufte, July 2000.

[20] Robert Venturi, Denise Scott Brown, and Steven Izenour, *Learning from Las Vegas* (Cambridge, 1977), 163.

decoration on a conventional shed the rather cynical and expensive distortion of program and structure to promote a duck. . . . It is now time to reevaluate the once-horrifying statement of John Ruskin that architecture is the decoration of construction, but we should append the warning of Pugin: It is all right to decorate construction but never construct decoration.[20]

Consider this unsavory exhibit at right—chockablock with cliché and stereotype, coarse humor, and a content-empty third dimension. It is the product of a visual sensitivity in which a thigh-graph with a fishnet-stocking grid counts as a Creative Concept. Everything counts, but nothing matters. The data-thin (and thus uncontextual) chart mixes up changes in the value of money with changes in diamond prices, a crucial confusion because the graph chronicles a time of high inflation.

Lurking behind chartjunk is contempt both for information and for the audience. Chartjunk promoters imagine that numbers and details are boring, dull, and tedious, requiring ornament to enliven. Cosmetic decoration, which frequently distorts the data, will never salvage an underlying lack of content.[21] If the numbers are boring, then you've got the wrong numbers. Credibility vanishes in clouds of chartjunk; who would trust a chart that looks like a video game?[22]

Worse is contempt for our audience, designing as if readers were obtuse and uncaring. In fact, consumers of graphics are often more intelligent about the information at hand than those who fabricate the data decoration. And, no matter what, the operating *moral* premise of information design should be that our readers are alert and caring; they may be busy, eager to get on with it, but they are not stupid. Clarity and simplicity are completely opposite simple-mindedness. Disrespect for the audience will leak through, damaging communication. What E. B. White said of writing is equally true for information design: "No

DIAMONDS *WERE* A GIRL'S BEST FRIEND
Average price of a one-carat D-flawless

$60,000
$50,000
$40,000
$30,000
$20,000

1978   1979   1980   1981   1982

[21] For detailed evidence, see Edward R. Tufte, *The Visual Display of Quantitative Information* (Cheshire, Connecticut, 1983), 52–87.

[22] Paul Rand writes, "Readers of a report should be unaware of its 'design.' Rather, they should be enticed into reading it by interesting content, logical arrangement and simple presentation. The printed page should appear natural and authoritative, avoiding gimmicks which might get in the way of its documentary character." Paul Rand, "Design," in *Speaking Out on Annual Reports* (New York, 1983).

one can write decently who is distrustful of the reader's intelligence, or whose attitude is patronizing."[23]

Standards of excellence for information design are set by *high quality maps*, with diverse bountiful detail, several layers of close reading combined with an overview, and rigorous data from engineering surveys. In contrast, the usual chartjunk performances look more like posters than maps. Posters are meant for viewing from a distance, with their strong images, large type, and thin data densities. Thus poster design provides very little counsel for making diagrams that are read more intensely. Display of closely-read data surely requires the skilled craft of good graphic and poster design: typography, object representation, layout, color, production techniques, and visual principles that inform criticism and revision. Too often those skills are accompanied by the ideology of chartjunk and data posterization; excellence in presenting information requires mastering the craft and spurning the ideology.[24]

THE ducks of information design are *false escapes from flatland*, adding pretend dimensions to impoverished data sets, merely fooling around with information. They don't work, just as this royal dining table, caught up in flatland, fails to hold the pots and plates. The king and queen watch in exasperation and exclaim, as their meal slides off, "It's the way they draw these wretched tables!"

[23] William Strunk, Jr. and E. B. White, *The Elements of Style* (New York, 1959), 70. An effective trial lawyer, Joe Jamail, noted "If you use too many pictures and make it like a circus or going to a matinee, jurors will think you think they're stupid." Susan Ayala, "Legal-Graphics Firms," *The Wall Street Journal*, July 21, 1988, 19.

[24] Our philosophy of information design—self-effacing displays intensely committed to rich data—parallels Balanchine's approach to dance. Lincoln Kirstein, in his 1972 essay "Balanchine's Fourth Dimension," describes an attitude governing the nature of dancing: "A committed Balanchine dancer (with a small 'd') comes to realize that Personality (with an enormous 'P') is a bundle of haphazard characteristics frozen in a pleasing mask for immediate identification and negotiable prestige. No matter what is danced—and it makes little difference—stardom dims the dancing. What is danced is perforce secondary. There are two types of ballet companies: those interested in selling stars and those occupied in demonstrating and extending the dance, as such. . . . Physicality in the tense relationships of Balanchine's dancers kept under so strict a discipline in so free an exercise pushes the spectacle to a high pressure point. Everything is so focused, compressed, packed, playful that it is as if the entire design were patterned on coiled steel or explosive fuels. Combinations of music in motion approach a fourth dimension that cannot be verbally defined." *Vogue*, 160 (December 1972), 118-129, 203-206; and Lincoln Kirstein, *Ballet: Bias and Belief* (New York, 1983), 111-119.

Harvey, *The Bulletin*, Sydney, Australia, ca. 1950s, as reproduced in E. H. Gombrich, *The Image and the Eye* (Oxford, 1982), 21.

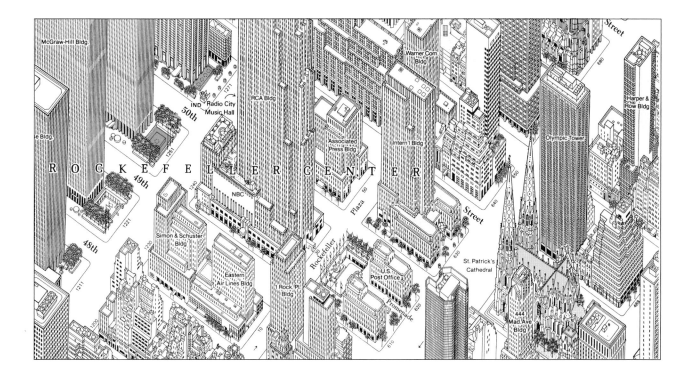

FOR 20 years Constantine Anderson refined this precise axonometric projection of midtown New York (shown here are Rockefeller Center environs), following the tradition of the classic 1739 Bretez-Turgot *Plan de Paris* (at left, the area around Pont Neuf and Notre Dame, from the 11th of 20 sheets). The Manhattan map embraces such fine points as individual windows, subway stations and bus shelters, telephone booths, building canopies, trees, and sidewalk planters. And the typography is persistently thorough; the entire map (60 by 92 centimeters, or 24 by 36 inches) reports 1,686 names of buildings, stores, and parks along with 657 specific street addresses—for a map, an abundant typographic density of 3 characters per square centimeter (20 per square inch). The only major concession to paper flatland is widening of the map's streets to reduce masking of some buildings by others.

This fine texture of exquisite detail leads to personal micro-readings, individual stories about the data: shops visited, hotels stayed at, walks taken, office windows at a floor worked on—all in the extended context of an entire building, street, and neighborhood.[1] Detail cumulates into larger coherent structures; those thousands of tiny windows, when seen at a distance, gray into surfaces to form a whole building. Simplicity of reading derives from the context of detailed and complex information, properly arranged. A most unconventional design strategy is revealed: *to clarify, add detail.*

Michel Etienne Turgot and Louis Bretez, *Plan de Paris* (Paris, 1739), plate II. Above, *The Isometric Map of Midtown Manhattan*, © 1989 The Manhattan Map Company.

[1] Italo Calvino's *Invisible Cities* (San Diego, 1974) records this texture of storied detail: cities are "relationships between the measurements of its space and the events of its past: the height of a lamp-post and the distance from the ground of a hanged usurper's swaying feet; the line strung from the lamp-post to the railing opposite and the festoons that decorate the course of the queen's nuptial procession; the height of that railing and the leap of the adulterer who climbed over it at dawn; the tilt of a guttering cat's progress along it as he slips into the same window; the firing range of a gunboat which has suddenly appeared beyond the cape and the bomb that destroys the guttering; the rips in the fishnet and the three old men seated on the dock mending nets and telling each other for the hundredth time the story of the gunboat of the usurper, who some say was the queen's illegitimate son, abandoned in his swaddling clothes there on the dock." On Calvino and maps, see a fine essay by Marc Treib, "Mapping Experience," *Design Quarterly*, 115 (1980).

A high-resolution aerial photograph of Senlis, one of the oldest cities in France (construction started on this Notre Dame cathedral in 1153), arrays micro-details mixing into overall pattern. Encircling Senlis was once a broad strip of Gallo-Roman fortification, now replaced by houses, arranged by the memory of the old town's plan. Such intensity of detail is routinely reported in photographs, so much data that digitizing these images for computers requires 10^6 to 10^8 bits.

Micro/macro composition also oversees this celebrated 1930 poster composed by the Soviet graphic artist Gustav Klutsis. The design and political point correspond—as the poster shows and also writes out, from collaborative work of many hands, one great plan will be fulfilled.

At work here is a critical and effective principle of information design. Panorama, vista, and prospect deliver to viewers the freedom of choice that derives from an overview, a capacity to compare and sort through detail. And that micro-information, like smaller texture in landscape perception, provides a credible refuge where the pace of visualization is condensed, slowed, and personalized.[2] These visual experiences are universal, rooted in human information-processing capacities and in the abundance and intricacy of everyday perceptions. Thus the power of micro/macro designs holds for every type of data display as well as for topographic views and landscape panoramas. Such designs can report immense detail, organizing complexity through multiple and (often) hierarchical layers of contextual reading.

Robert Cameron, *Above Paris* (San Francisco, 1984), 146–147.

[2] Jay Appleton, *The Experience of Landscape* (Chichester, 1975); John A. Jakle, *The Visual Elements of Landscape* (Amherst, 1987).

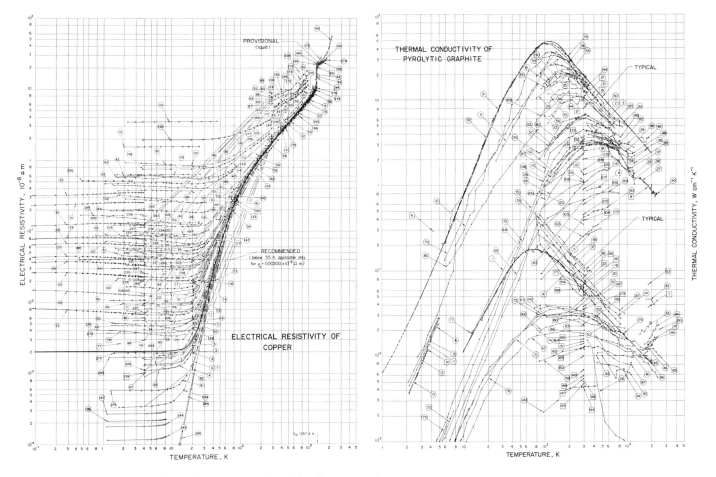

These multi-layered graphs report a clouded relationship between temperature and conductivity for various elements, as measured by many different laboratories. Each set of connected points comes from a single publication, cited by an identification number. Note how easily these displays organize the material, recording observations from several hundred studies and also enforcing comparisons among quite divergent results (this is science?) scattered around the correct curve, a solid line labeled RECOMMENDED. Since both scales are logarithmic, cycling through 3.5 to 6 orders of magnitude, deviations from the recommended curve are often quite substantial. In this micro/macro arrangement, 4 layers of data are placed in evidence—individual points measured within each study, connected curves formed by those results, and, finally, an overall conglomeration of curves (which are compared with the standard).

Still another slice of data can be added. A number, linked to an *alphabetical* list ordered by author's name, now identifies each published paper. A better method is to order the list by the *date* of publication; then the numerical codes correspond to the sequence of findings—for example, 61c indicates the third paper published in 1961. This graphical indexing depicts which study first had the right answer, and movement toward the correct curve can be tracked over the years.

R. A. Matula, "Electrical Resistivity of Copper, Gold, Palladium, and Silver," *Journal of Physical and Chemical Reference Data*, 8 (1979), 1162; C. Y. Ho, R. W. Powell, and P. E. Liley, *Thermal Conductivity of the Elements. Journal of Physical and Chemical Reference Data*, 3 (1974), 1-151, 1-244.

These extraordinary statistical maps report data for thousands of tiny grid squares (1 km on a side). Below, a map of Tokyo shows population density; note smaller concentrations dotting the tracks radiating from the city, as people cluster along rail lines and station stops. At this level of detail, residents can find their own particular square and also see it in a broader context. The map at right records the proportion of children living at each location, with a systematic pattern of lower percentages in central Tokyo (where space is limited and costly) and a suburban ring teeming—relatively—with children. A bright idea lies behind these grid-square or mesh maps. Conventional blot maps (choropleth maps,

Statistics Bureau, Prime Minister's Office, *Statistical Maps on Grid Square Basis: The 1980 Population Census Results* (Tokyo, 1985). See Hidenori Kimura, "Grid Square Statistics for the Distribution and Mobility of Population in Japan," Statistics Bureau (Tokyo, no date), manuscript.

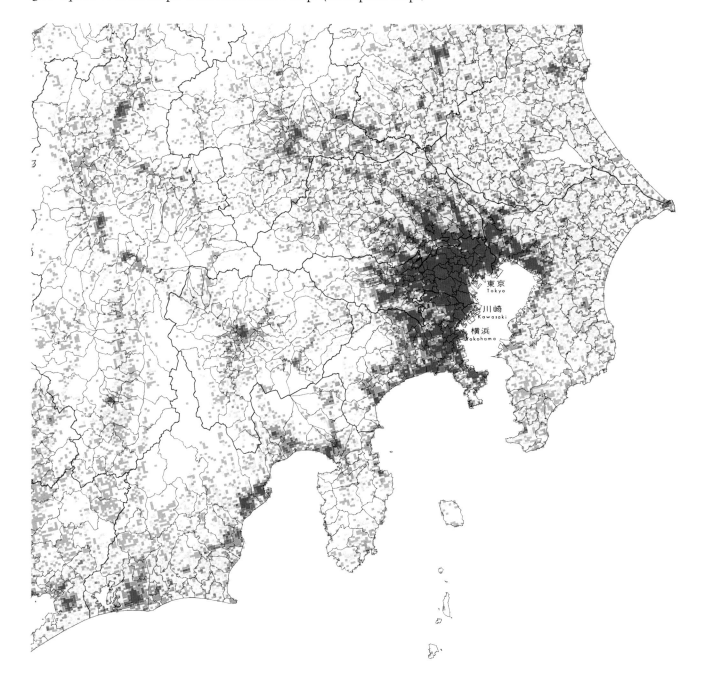

in the jargon) paint over areas formed by *given* geographic or political boundaries. The consequences are (1) sizes of areas are non-uniform, (2) colored-in areas are proportional to (often nearly empty) land areas instead of the activities depicted, with large unpopulated areas often receiving greatest visual emphasis, and (3) historical changes in political boundaries disrupt continuity of statistical comparisons.[3] Mesh maps finesse these problems. For these maps, the whole country of Japan was divided up in 379,000 equal-sized units and then, in a heroic endeavor, census data and addresses were collated to match the new grid squares. Arbitrary but statistically wise boundaries now cradle the micro-data.

[3] J. C. Müller, "Wahrheit und Lüge in Thematischen Karten—Zur Problematik der Darstellung Statistischer Sachverhalte," *Kartographische Nachrichten*, 35-2 (1985), 44-52. Other uses of mesh maps include describing flows; see Waldo R. Tobler, "A Model of Geographic Movement," *Geographical Analysis*, 13 (January 1981), 1-19.

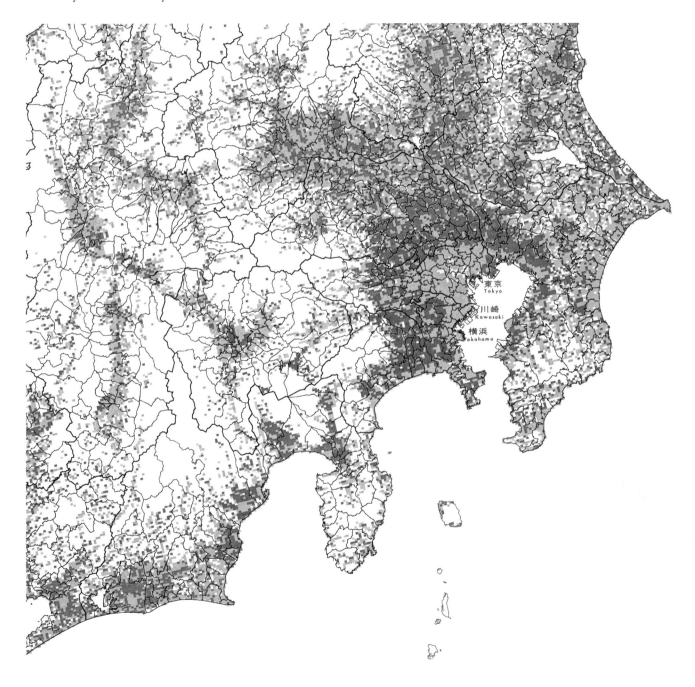

THE Vietnam Veterans Memorial in Washington, DC achieves its visual and emotional strength by means of micro/macro design. From a distance the entire collection of names of 58,000 dead soldiers arrayed on the black granite yields a visual measure of what 58,000 means, as the letters of each name blur into a gray shape, cumulating to the final toll. When a viewer approaches, these shapes resolve into individual names. Some of the living seek the name of one particular soldier in a personal micro-reading; more than a few visitors here touch the etched, textured names. We focus on the tragic information; absent are the big porticoes, steps and stairs, and other marble paraphernalia usually attached to grand official monuments. Walking on a slight grade downward (approaching from either side), our first close reading is of panels no higher than a few names. But looking forward, the visitor sees names of the dead rising higher and higher, a statistical blur of marks in the distance with micro-detail at hand. The context is enlarged by calm reflections off polished black granite, reflections of the living and of trees, and, at a distance, of the Lincoln and Washington memorials toward which the walls angle.

An additional data dimension comes from the *ordering* of names. The memorial's designer, Maya Ying Lin, proposed that names be listed by date of death rather than alphabetically:

> . . . chronological listing was essential to her design. War veterans would find their story told, and their friends remembered, in the panel that corresponded with their tour of duty in Vietnam. Locating specific names with the aid of a directory would be like finding bodies on a battlefield. . . . Some initially disagreed. If 58,000 names were scattered along the wall, anyone looking for a specific name would wander around for hours and then leave in frustration. One solution seemed obvious: list everyone in alphabetical order. . . . But when a two-inch-thick Defense Department listing of Vietnam casualties was examined, thinking changed. There were over 600 Smiths; 16 people named James Jones had died in Vietnam. Alphabetical listing would make the Memorial look like a telephone book engraved in granite, destroying the sense of unique loss that each name carried. . . . [4]

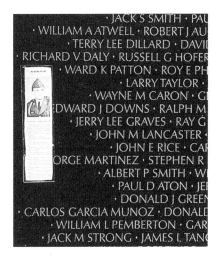

[4] Jan C. Scruggs and Joel L. Swerdlow, *To Heal A Nation: The Vietnam Veterans Memorial* (New York, 1985), 78–79. See Jeffrey Karl Ochsner, "A Space of Loss: The Vietnam Veterans Memorial," *Journal of Architectural Education*, 50 (February 1997), 156–171; and Maya Lin, "Making the Memorial," *The New York Review of Books*, 47 (November 2, 2000), 33–35.

Vietnam Veterans Memorial, *Directory of Names* (Washington, DC, 1985). Shown here is an excerpt from the finder, a large book recording the name, rank, service, birthdate, deathdate, home town, and panel and line number locating each name on the stone memorial.

SMITH ROBERT GEORGE	PFC	AR	11 JUN 45	02 JAN 66	CLEVELAND	OH	4E	52
SMITH ROBERT HAROLD	SP4	AR	27 OCT 46	24 JAN 67	WARMINSTER	PA	14E	73
SMITH ROBERT JAMES	SSGT	AR	16 DEC 45	18 APR 68	ALBANY	NY	50E	41
SMITH ROBERT JEREMIAH	CPL	AR	16 MAY 47	29 SEP 67	BUFFALO	NY	27E	32
SMITH ROBERT JOE	SP4	AR	04 JUL 44	21 MAR 67	JACKSONVILLE	FL	17E	14
SMITH ROBERT JOHN	A1C	AF	15 OCT 42	25 JUN 65	SCARBORO	ME	2E	19
SMITH ROBERT JOSEPH	PFC	MC	04 AUG 48	26 AUG 68	COLUMBUS	GA	46W	34
SMITH ROBERT JR	PFC	AR	20 MAR 45	26 MAY 66	PHILADELPHIA	PA	7E	111
SMITH ROBERT L	SGT	AR	30 JUN 37	25 AUG 66	MILLINGTON	TN	10E	44
SMITH ROBERT LEE	SP4	AR	06 NOV 43	29 JAN 66	WELCH	WV	4E	115
SMITH ROBERT LEE	SSGT	AR	22 AUG 32	25 MAY 68	CHILLICOTHE	OH	67W	6
SMITH ROBERT LEE	LCPL	MC	09 JAN 46	31 MAY 68	MONROE	MI	62W	17
SMITH ROBERT LEE	PFC	MC	28 MAR 46	02 SEP 68	CINCINNATI	OH	45W	28
SMITH ROBERT LEE	PFC	AR	06 OCT 43	30 DEC 69	CHICAGO	IL	15W	111
SMITH ROBERT LEE JR	LCPL	MC	31 JUL 45	04 MAR 66	NEWPORT NEWS	VA	5E	110
SMITH ROBERT LEWIS	PFC	AR	05 APR 48	06 JUN 68	SMITHLAND	KY	59W	15
SMITH ROBERT LINDO	PFC	AR	22 JAN 40	17 FEB 66	SANFORD	NC	5E	43
SMITH ROBERT LOUIS	CPL	AR	27 MAY 47	08 MAR 67	ANGIER	NC	16E	42
SMITH ROBERT MICHAEL	SGT	AR	11 NOV 48	10 MAR 70	PEORIA	IL	13W	108

SMITH ROBERT NORMAN	COL	MC	20 SEP 26	19 AUG 69	TRUCKSVILLE	PA	19W	74
SMITH ROBERT SR	SGT	AR	28 MAY 32	21 OCT 66	ALEXANDRIA	LA	11E	96
SMITH ROBERT T	SGT	AR	01 AUG 44	12 APR 69	INDIANAPOLIS	IN	27W	67
SMITH ROBERT WALTER	SGT	AR	27 APR 47	20 JAN 69	LAKE CORMORANT	MS	34W	45
SMITH ROBERT WILBUR	CAPT	AF	02 JUL 44	17 APR 70	WASHINGTON	DC	11W	19
SMITH ROBERT WILLIAM	PFC	AR	02 AUG 47	12 NOV 66	WENTZVILLE	MO	12E	64
SMITH RODNEY HOWE	LTC	AR	02 AUG 31	03 JUN 67	ARLINGTON	VA	21E	53
SMITH ROGER LEE	SP4	AR	14 MAR 47	03 OCT 68	SOUTH POINT	OH	41W	2
SMITH RONALD C	SP4	AR	21 APR 46	03 MAR 67	DEARBORN	MI	16E	14
SMITH RONALD CARLTON	SP4	AR	18 SEP 44	14 APR 68	HATBORO	PA	50E	1
SMITH RONALD EUGENE	SFC	AR	29 MAR 40	28 NOV 70	COVINGTON	IN	6W	89
SMITH RONALD ORDON	SP4	AR	03 JUN 47	21 NOV 67	COVINGTON	TN	30E	60
SMITH RONALD LARRY	1LT	MC	02 MAR 36	23 FEB 69	HOGANSVILLE	GA	31W	24
SMITH RONALD LEE	PFC	AR	20 DEC 47	26 MAY 68	BEECH GROVE	IN	65W	1
SMITH RONNIE WAYNE	PFC	MC	28 SEP 48	28 MAY 68	HUNTSVILLE	AL	64W	16
SMITH RONNY	PFC	MC	04 FEB 49	10 MAY 69	LENA	MS	25W	43
SMITH ROY	CPL	MC	11 MAY 46	20 MAY 67	BIRMINGHAM	AL	20E	65
SMITH ROY MILTON	SP4	AR	31 MAR 50	19 FEB 71	HOUSTON	TX	5W	122

Thus the names on stone triple-function: to memorialize each person who died, to make a mark adding up the total, and to indicate sequence and approximate date of death. A directory-book alphabetically lists all the names and serves as a finder, pointing viewers to the location of a single engraved name.

The spirit of the *individual* created by the wall—both of each death and of each viewer personally editing—decisively affects how we see other visitors. The busloads of tourists appear not so much as crowds but rather as many separate individual faces, not as interruptions at an architectural performance but rather as our colleagues.[5]

[5] Since installation in 1982, the Vietnam Memorial has become one of the most visited monuments in Washington. Some four million people saw it in 1988, according to "Maya Lin's Unwavering Vision," *The Washington Post*, February 13, 1989, B1, B6. In 1991, the sculptor Chris Burden created "The Other Vietnam Memorial," an attempt to list the three million Vietnamese killed during the war. See Robert Storr, *Dislocations* (Museum of Modern Art, New York, 1991), 42-47.

GRAPHICAL timetables also exemplify the multiplicity and wholeness of micro/macro design. Described here is the overall structure of a railroad system, as the individual lines aggregate into systematic patterns. This computer-graphical timetable shown here governs Japanese high-speed trains, or *Shinkansen*. Station stops are plotted down the side of the grid; time of day runs across the top; diagonal lines show the space-time path of each train. The Tokyo control room directing these high-speed trains is filled with these graphical timetables, long paper strips used to help oversee thousands of journeys each day—a task which makes clear the enormous advantages of *seeing* information rather than tabulating data. Similar charts are also used for planning new schedules, with different interest groups negotiating where a train should stop and the frequency of service as they design a graphical timetable.[6]

[6] Hiroaki Shigehara, *Ressha Daiya* [Train Diagram] (Tokyo, 1983). An enchanting story of graphical timetable design is told by Hideo Ohki, "Transportation of Professional Baseball Spectators by Seibu Railways," *Japanese Railway Engineering*, 19 (1979), 19-23, describing a small railway serving baseball spectators. Considerations include irregular length of games, and spectators leaving early in event of a runaway. Railway workers monitor the game on television in order to adjust dynamically the train graph (as it is called, in a logic so visual that the graph entirely replaces entabled times).

Operation diagram for 12:00 noon, July 25, 1985, Tokaido and Sanyo Shinkansen Lines (bullet train), Japanese National Railroad control room, Tokyo.

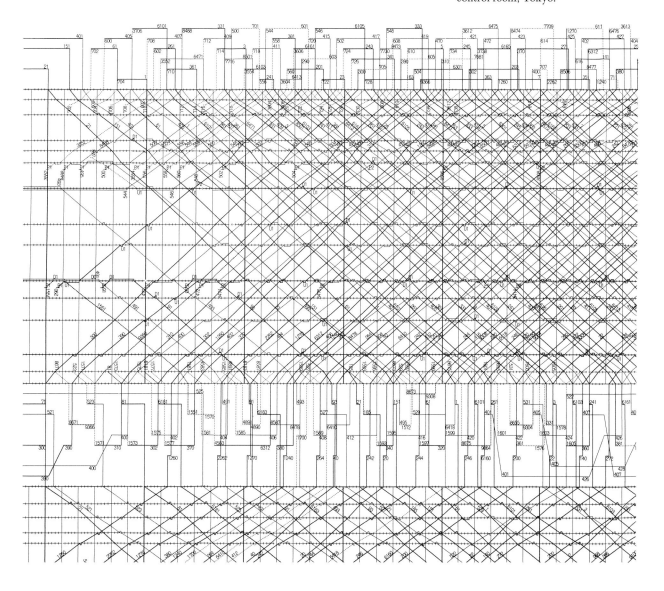

Stem-and-leaf plots of statistical analysis also rely on micro/macro design. Each data point simultaneously states its value and fills a space representing one counted unit, like the names on the Vietnam Veterans Memorial, with those spaces in turn assembling to form a profile of the overall univariate distribution. Envisioned here are the heights of 218 volcanoes; each individual number helps to build the histogram. Micro-

0 | 9 = 900 feet	0	98766562
	1	97719630
	2	6998776654442211009850
	3	876655412099551426
	4	9998844331929433361107
	5	9766666655442210097731
	6	898665441077761065
	7	98855431100652108073
	8	653322122937
	9	377655421000493
	10	0984433165212
Stem-and-leaf displays:	11	4963201631
heights of 218 volcanoes, unit 100 feet.	12	45421164
	13	47830
	14	00
	15	676
	16	52
	17	92
	18	5
19 | 3 = 19,300 feet	19	39730

data has replaced the information-empty bars of a traditional barchart. This idea of making each graphical element *repeatedly* effective animated design of the stem-and-leaf plot. In describing his invention, John Tukey wrote: "If we are going to make a mark, it may as well be a meaningful one. The simplest—and most useful—meaningful mark is a digit."[7]

In a similar fashion, this train schedule below positions the individual departure times so that they add up to a frequency distribution. For trains that run often, leading hour-digits need not be repeated over and over, and, instead, minutes can be stacked:

[7] John W. Tukey, "Some Graphic and Semigraphic Displays," in T. A. Bancroft, ed., *Statistical Papers in Honor of George W. Snedecor* (Ames, Iowa, 1972), 296.

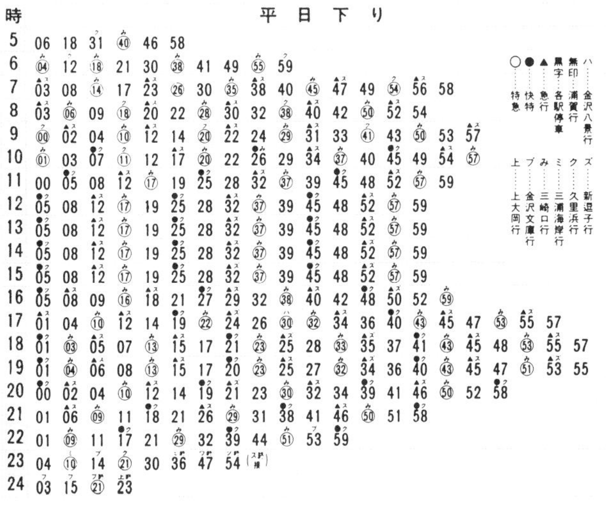

時　　　　　　　平　日　下　り

5	06 18 31 40 46 58
6	04 12 18 21 30 38 41 49 55 59
7	03 08 14 17 23 26 30 35 38 40 45 47 49 54 56 58
8	03 06 09 18 20 22 28 30 32 38 40 42 50 52 54
9	00 02 04 10 12 14 20 22 24 29 31 33 41 43 50 53 57
10	01 03 07 11 12 17 20 22 26 29 34 37 40 45 49 54 57
11	00 05 08 12 17 19 25 28 32 37 39 45 48 52 57 59
12	05 08 12 17 19 25 28 32 37 39 45 48 52 57 59
13	05 08 12 17 19 25 28 32 37 39 45 48 52 57 59
14	05 08 12 17 19 25 28 32 37 39 45 48 52 57 59
15	05 08 12 17 19 25 28 32 37 39 45 48 52 57 59
16	05 08 09 16 18 21 27 29 32 38 40 42 48 50 52 59
17	01 04 10 12 14 19 22 24 26 30 32 34 36 40 43 45 48 53 55 57
18	01 03 05 07 14 17 21 25 28 32 34 36 40 43 45 48 53 55 57
19	01 04 06 08 13 15 17 20 23 25 27 32 34 36 40 43 45 47 51 53 55
20	00 02 04 10 12 14 19 21 23 30 32 34 39 41 46 50 52 58
21	01 06 09 11 18 21 26 29 31 38 41 46 50 51 58
22	01 09 11 17 21 29 32 39 44 51 53 59
23	04 10 14 21 30 36 47 54
24	03 15 21 23

Keihin Express Line at Yokohama Station, Sagami Tetsudo Company, 1985 timetable, 76. Encodings indicate types of trains (super express, commuter, and so on) and various local stops.

Reported is the overall time distribution of 292 daily trains, with peaks during morning and evening rush hours. The shrewd design saves 777 characters, avoiding this typographical extravaganza below, which lacks the intensive annotation of the stem-and-leaf original and also fails to provide clear testimony about frequency of train service by hour.[8]

[8] The stem-and-leaf schedule contains 619 numbers; the typographic version 1,396 numbers and periods. Thus the stem-and-leaf schedule saves 777 characters, and, more importantly, gives a much a better sense of comparison of train times.

5.06	7.17	8.28	9.31	10.40	11.57	13.12	14.28	15.45	16.52	17.53	18.45	19.40	20.39	21.51	23.36
5.18	7.23	8.30	9.33	10.45	11.59	13.17	14.32	15.48	16.59	17.55	18.48	19.43	20.41	21.58	23.47
5.31	7.26	8.32	9.41	10.49	12.05	13.19	14.37	15.52	17.01	17.57	18.53	19.45	20.46	22.01	23.54
5.40	7.30	8.38	9.43	10.54	12.08	13.25	14.39	15.57	17.04	18.01	18.55	19.47	20.50	22.09	24.03
5.46	7.35	8.40	9.50	10.57	12.12	13.28	14.45	15.59	17.10	18.03	18.57	19.51	20.52	22.11	24.15
5.58	7.38	8.42	9.53	11.00	12.17	13.32	14.48	16.05	17.12	18.05	19.01	19.53	20.58	22.17	24.21
6.04	7.40	8.50	9.57	11.05	12.19	13.37	14.52	16.08	17.14	18.07	19.04	19.55	21.01	22.21	24.23
6.12	7.45	8.52	10.01	11.08	12.25	13.39	14.57	16.09	17.19	18.13	19.06	20.00	21.06	22.29	
6.18	7.47	8.54	10.03	11.12	12.28	13.45	14.59	16.16	17.22	18.15	19.08	20.02	21.09	22.32	
6.21	7.49	9.00	10.07	11.17	12.32	13.48	15.05	16.18	17.24	18.17	19.13	20.04	21.11	22.39	
6.30	7.54	9.02	10.11	11.19	12.37	13.52	15.08	16.21	17.26	18.21	19.15	20.10	21.18	22.44	
6.38	7.56	9.04	10.12	11.25	12.39	13.57	15.12	16.27	17.30	18.23	19.17	20.12	21.21	22.51	
6.41	7.58	9.10	10.17	11.28	12.45	13.59	15.17	16.29	17.32	18.25	19.20	20.14	21.26	22.53	
6.49	8.03	9.12	10.20	11.32	12.48	14.05	15.19	16.32	17.34	18.28	19.23	20.19	21.29	22.59	
6.55	8.06	9.14	10.22	11.37	12.52	14.08	15.25	16.38	17.36	18.33	19.25	20.21	21.31	23.04	
6.59	8.09	9.20	10.26	11.39	12.57	14.12	15.28	16.40	17.40	18.35	19.27	20.23	21.38	23.10	
7.03	8.18	9.22	10.29	11.45	12.59	14.17	15.32	16.42	17.43	18.37	19.32	20.30	21.41	23.14	
7.08	8.20	9.24	10.34	11.48	13.05	14.19	15.37	16.48	17.45	18.41	19.34	20.32	21.46	23.21	
7.14	8.22	9.29	10.37	11.52	13.08	14.25	15.39	16.50	17.47	18.43	19.36	20.34	21.50	23.30	

In all these micro/macro designs, the same ink serves more than one informational purpose; graphical elements are multifunctioning. This suggests a missed opportunity in the stem-and-leaf timetable—surely leaves of numbers can grow from *both* sides of a central stem. And so it is; the finely detailed timetable below records trains running in several directions from the station, with the platforms 7–8 at left and platforms 5–6 at right (at the arrows, note how numbers serpentine around a bend when times for the morning rush hour exceed the grid). Sometimes this arrangement is called a "back to back stem-and-leaf plot." Nonetheless, Japanese train passengers have managed to use the schedules for decades without ever knowing the fancy name.

Tokaido Line at Yokohama Station, Sagami Tetsudo Company, 1985 timetable, 72.

EACH at least as big as this drawing of the earth, some 7,000 pieces of space debris—operating and dead satellites, explosion fragments from rocket engines, garbage bags and frozen sewage dumped by astronauts, shrapnel from antisatellite weapons tests, 34 nuclear reactors and their fuel cores, an escaped wrench and a toothbrush—now orbit our world. Only about 5 percent are working satellites. By means of extraordinary data recording and analysis, military computers identify and then track *each* of these 7,000 objects (≥10 cm in diameter), in order to differentiate the debris from a missile attack, for which we may be thankful. Space is not totally self-cleaning; some of the stuff will be up there for centuries, endangering people and satellites working in space as well as inducing spurious astronomical observations. The risk of a damaging collision is perhaps 1 in 500 during several years in orbit. The volume of debris has doubled about every 5 years; future testing of space weapons will accelerate the trashing of space.[9]

[9] Donald J. Kessler and Burton G. Cour-Palais, "Collision Frequency of Artificial Satellites: The Creation of a Debris Belt," *Journal of Geophysical Research*, 83 (June 1, 1978), 2637-2646; Donald J. Kessler, "Earth Orbital Pollution," in Eugene C. Hargrove, ed., *Beyond Spaceship Earth* (San Francisco, 1986), 47-65; Nicholas L. Johnson, "History and Consequences of On-orbit Break-ups," in *Space Debris, Asteroids and Satellite Orbits*, D. J. Kessler, E. Grün, and L. Sehnal, eds., *Advances in Space Research*, 5 (Oxford, 1985), 11-19; Eliot Marshall, "Space Junk Grows with Weapons Tests," *Science*, 230 (October 25, 1985), 424-425; Joel R. Primack, "Gamma-Ray Observations of Orbiting Nuclear Reactors," *Science*, 244 (April 28, 1989), 407-408.

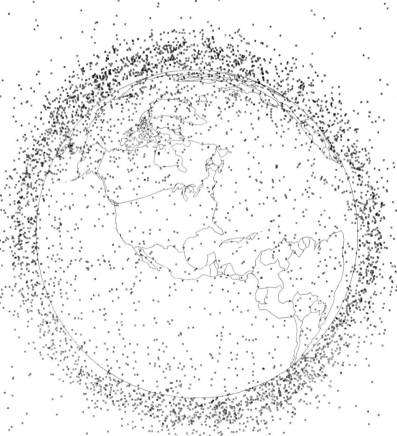

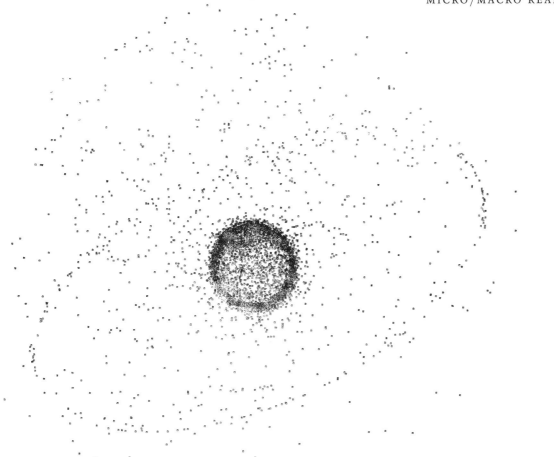

The consequences (as of 0:00 hours Universal time, July 1, 1987) are shown in these phenomenal and disheartening micro/macro images, as a multiplicity of 7,000 dots adds to the overall pattern of orbital pollution. Most of the debris is relatively close to earth; a more distant view shows a ring formed by geosynchronous satellites. Not shown are some 50,000 smaller objects (size between 1 cm and 10 cm), as well as 10 billion to 100 billion paint chips now in orbit.

NEARLY all micro/macro designs of this chapter have portrayed large quantities of data at high densities, up to thousands of bits per square centimeter and 20 million bits per page, pushing the limits of printing technology. Such quantities are thoroughly familiar, although hardly noticed: the human eye registers 150 million bits, the 35 mm slide some 25 million bits, conventional large-scale topographic maps up to 150 million bits, the color screen of a small personal computer 8 million bits. Typographic densities are also substantial; a few reference books report 28,000 characters per page, books on non-fiction best-seller lists from 5,000 to 15,000 characters per page, and the world's telephone books run between 10,000 and 18,000 characters per page. Statistical graphics and other information displays should do so well.

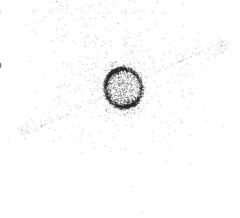

Illustrations provided by Nicholas L. Johnson, Teledyne Brown Engineering, Colorado Springs, Colorado. Dots are not to scale of Earth.

We thrive in information-thick worlds because of our marvelous and everyday capacities to select, edit, single out, structure, highlight, group, pair, merge, harmonize, synthesize, focus, organize, condense, reduce, boil down, choose, categorize, catalog, classify, list, abstract, scan, look into, idealize, isolate, discriminate, distinguish, screen, pigeonhole, pick over, sort, integrate, blend, inspect, filter, lump, skip, smooth, chunk, average, approximate, cluster, aggregate, outline, summarize, itemize, review, dip into, flip through, browse, glance into, leaf through, skim, refine, enumerate, glean, synopsize, winnow the wheat from the chaff, and separate the sheep from the goats. And a lot of data are processed: recent evidence indicates that the optic nerve connecting eye's retina to brain operates at 10 Mb per second, equivalent to an Ethernet.[10]

Visual displays rich with data are not only an appropriate and proper complement to human capabilities, but also such designs are frequently optimal. If the visual task is contrast, comparison, and choice—as so often it is—then the more relevant information within eyespan, the better. Vacant, low-density displays, the dreaded posterization of data spread over pages and pages, require viewers to rely on visual memory— a weak skill—to make a contrast, a comparison, a choice.

Micro/macro designs enforce both local and global comparisons and, at the same time, avoid the disruption of context switching. All told, exactly what is needed for reasoning about information.[11]

High-density designs also allow viewers to select, to narrate, to recast and personalize data for their own uses. Thus control of information is given over to *viewers*, not to editors, designers, or decorators. Data-thin, forgetful displays move viewers toward ignorance and passivity, and at the same time diminish the credibility of the source. Thin data rightly prompts suspicions: "What are they leaving out? Is that really everything they know? What are they hiding? Is that all they did?" Now and then it is claimed that vacant space is "friendly" (anthropomorphizing an inherently murky idea) but *it is not how much empty space there is, but rather how it is used. It is not how much information there is, but rather how effectively it is arranged.*

Showing complexity often demands hard, thoughtful work. Detailed micro/macro designs have substantial costs for data collection, design, custom computing, image processing, and production—expenses similar to that of first-class cartography. But once there's a good template, intense data flows can be managed routinely, as the initial front-end investment in design is repaid by a great longrun template. And the usual economies of declining costs for each additional data packet may well persist. One excellent high-resolution data display image can replace 20 scattered slides. And our readers might keep that one really informative image, although they will surely discard those twenty slides and all their chartjunk, administrative debris, and empty space.

[10] Kristin Koch, Judith McLean, Ronen Segev, Michael A. Freed, Michael J. Berry, Vijay Balasubramanian, Peter Sterling, "How Much the Eye Tells the Brain," *Current Biology* 16 (July 25, 2006), 1428-1434.

[11] In user interfaces for computers, a problem undermining information exchange between human and software is "constant *context switches.* By this we mean that the user is not presented with one basic display format and one uniform style of interaction, but instead, with frequent changes: A scatterplot is present; it goes away, and is replaced by a menu; the menu goes away, and is replaced by the scatterplot; and so on. While the menu is present, the user cannot see the scatterplot, and vice versa. This means that users constantly have to adjust to a changing visual environment rather than focusing on the data. The user is also forced to remember things seen in one view so that he or she can use the other view effectively. This means that the user's short-term memory is occupied with the incidentals rather than with the significant issues of analysis." Andrew W. Donoho, David L. Donoho, and Miriam Gasko, "MacSpin: Dynamic Graphics on a Desktop Computer," *Computer Graphics & Applications* (July 1988), 58.

What about confusing clutter? Information overload? Doesn't data have to be "boiled down" and "simplified"? These common questions miss the point, for the quantity of detail is an issue completely separate from the difficulty of reading. *Clutter and confusion are failures of design, not attributes of information.* Often the less complex and less subtle the line, the more ambiguous and less interesting is the reading. Stripping the detail out of data is a style based on personal preference and fashion, considerations utterly indifferent to substantive content. What Josef Albers wrote about typography is true for information design:

> The concept that "the simpler the form of a letter the simpler its reading" was an obsession of beginning constructivism. It became something like a dogma, and is still followed by "modernistic" typographers.
>
> This notion has proved to be wrong, because in reading we do not read letters but words, words as a whole, as a "word picture." Ophthalmology has disclosed that the more the letters are differentiated from each other, the easier is the reading.
>
> Without going into comparisons and the details, it should be realized that words consisting of only capital letters present the most difficult reading—because of their equal height, equal volume, and, with most, their equal width. When comparing serif letters with sans-serif, the latter provide an uneasy reading. The fashionable preference for sans-serif in text shows neither historical nor practical competence.[12]

So much for the conventional, facile, and false equation: simpleness of data and design = clarity of reading. Simpleness is another aesthetic preference, not an information display strategy, not a guide to clarity. What we seek instead is a rich texture of data, a comparative context, an understanding of complexity revealed with an economy of means.

Robert Venturi opens his *Complexity and Contradiction in Architecture* with a broad extension of Albers' point:

> I like complexity and contradiction in architecture. . . . I speak of a complex and contradictory architecture based on the richness and ambiguity of modern experience, including that experience which is inherent in art. Everywhere, except in architecture, complexity and contradiction have been acknowledged, from Gödel's proof of inconsistency in mathematics to T. S. Eliot's analysis of "difficult" poetry and Joseph Albers' definition of the paradoxical quality of painting. . . . Architects can no longer afford to be intimidated by the puritanically moral language of orthodox Modern architecture . . . . an architecture of complexity and contradiction has a special obligation toward the whole: its truth must be in its totality or its implications of totality. It must embody the difficult unity of inclusion rather than the easy unity of exclusion. . . . Where simplicity cannot work, simpleness results. Blatant simplification means bland architecture. Less is a bore. [13]

But, finally, the deepest reason for displays that portray complexity and intricacy is that the worlds we seek to understand are complex and intricate. "God is in the details," said Mies van der Rohe, capturing the essential quality of micro/macro performances.

[12] Josef Albers, *Interaction of Color* (New Haven, 1963; revised edition, 1975), 4.

[13] Robert Venturi, *Complexity and Contradiction in Architecture* (New York, 1966), 16-17.

「悲」の長い横画は流動
感に変化を与えている

「へ」の極端に短かい横画は意表
をついて変化の美を出している

「悲」の長い横画は流動
感に変化を与えている

「へ」の極端に短かい横画は意表
をついて変化の美を出している

3 *Layering and Separation*

In ghostlier demarcations, keener sounds.
Wallace Stevens, *The Idea of Order at Key West*

CONFUSION and clutter are failures of design, not attributes of information. And so the point is to find design strategies that reveal detail and complexity—rather than to fault the data for an excess of complication. Or, worse, to fault viewers for a lack of understanding. Among the most powerful devices for reducing noise and enriching the content of displays is the technique of layering and separation, visually stratifying various aspects of the data.

Effective layering of information is often difficult; for every excellent performance, a hundred clunky spectacles arise. An omnipresent, yet subtle, design issue is involved: the various elements collected together on flatland *interact*, creating non-information patterns and texture simply through their combined presence. Josef Albers described this visual effect as 1 + 1 = *3 or more*, when two elements show themselves along with assorted incidental by-products of their partnership—occasionally a basis for pleasing aesthetic effects but always a continuing danger to data exhibits.[1] Such patterns become dynamically obtrusive when our displays leave the relative constancy of paper and move to the changing video flatland of computer terminals. There, all sorts of unplanned and lushly cluttered interacting combinations turn up, with changing layers of information arrayed in miscellaneous windows surrounded by a frame of system commands and other computer administrative debris.

[1] Josef Albers, "One Plus One Equals Three or More: Factual Facts and Actual Facts," in Albers, *Search Versus Re-Search* (Hartford, 1969), 17-18.

AT left a second color annotates the brush strokes of the calligrapher, Uboku Nishitani. By creating a distinct layer, the red commentary maintains detail, coherence, and serenity, in a crisp precision side-by-side with a gestural and expressive black line in this marriage of color and information. The saturated quality of the red partially offsets its lighter value and finer line (appropriate to meticulous annotation). Alone, each color makes a strong statement; together, a stronger one.

Uboku Nishitani, *Koyagire Daiishu* [*The First Seed of Koyagiri*], volume 17 of *Shodo Giho Koza* [*Techniques in Calligraphy*] (Tokyo, 1972), 56. Redrawn.

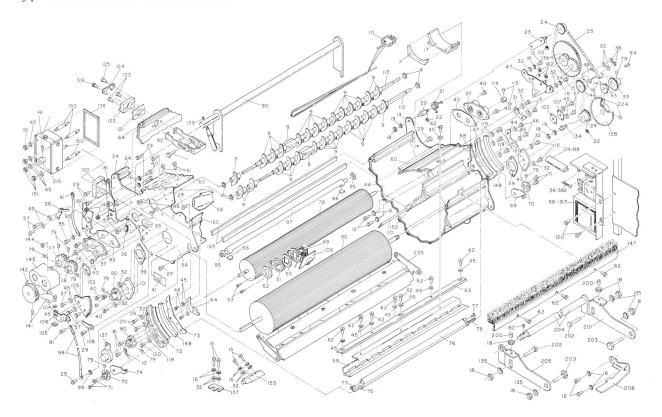

Similarly, color effortlessly differentiates between annotation and annotated, in this skillful industrial-strength diagram separating 300 small parts and their identifying numbers.

What matters—inevitably, unrelentingly—is the proper *relationship* among information layers. These visual relationships must be in relevant proportion and in harmony to the substance of the ideas, evidence, and data conveyed. "Proportion and harmony" need not be vague counsel; their meanings are revealed in the practice of detailed visual editing of data displays. For example, in this train timetable a heavy-handed grid interacts with the type, generating a stripy texture and fighting with the scheduled times. The prominent top position in the table shows the least important information, a four-digit train identifier used by railroad personnel and nobody else:

IBM Series III Copier/Duplicator, Adjustment Parts Manual (Boulder, Colorado, 1976), 101. Drawn by Gary E. Graham.

New Jersey Transit, *Northeastern Corridor Timetable* (Newark, 1985).

Train No.	3701	XM 3301	3801	A 67	3 3803	3 3201	A3 51	.3 3703	3 3807	3 3203	A3 61	3 3809	A3 47	3 3901	3 3811	3 3903	3 3813	3205	3815	3817	3819	3207	3821	3823	3825	.3209	3827	3829	3831
	A.M.	A.M.	A.M.	A.M.	A.M.	A.M.	A.M.	A.M.	A.M.	A.M.	A.M.	A.M.	A.M.	A.M.	A.M.	A.M.	A.M.	A.M.	A.M.	A.M.	A.M.	A.M.	A.M.	A.M.	A.M.	A.M.	P.M.	P.M.	P.M.
New York, N.Y.	12.10	12.40	1.30	3.52	4.50	6.10	6.25	6.35	6.50	7.10	7.30	7.33	7.45	7.50	8.05	8.25	8.40	8.50	9.10	9.40	10.10	10.25	10.40	11.10	11.40	11.50	12.10	12.40	1.10
Newark, N.J. P	12.24	12.55	1.44	4.07	5.04	6.24	6.38	6.49	7.04	7.24	7.45	7.47	7.59	8.04	8.19	8.39	8.54	9.04	9.24	9.54	10.24	10.39	10.54	11.24	11.54	12.04	12.24	12.54	1.24
North Elizabeth	....	....	....	....	....	....	....	....	....	7.30	....	....	....	8.10	....	....	....	....	....	....	....	....	....	....	....	....	....	....	....
Elizabeth	12.31	1.03	1.51	....	5.11	6.31	....	6.56	7.11	7.32	....	7.54	....	8.13	8.26	8.46	9.01	9.11	9.31	10.01	10.31	10.46	11.01	11.31	12.01	12.11	12.31	1.01	1.31
Linden	12.36	....	1.56	....	5.16	6.36	....	7.01	7.15	7.37	....	7.59	....	8.18	8.31	8.51	9.06	....	9.36	10.06	10.36	....	11.06	11.36	12.06	....	12.36	1.06	1.36
North Rahway	....	....	....	....	....	....	....	7.03	....	7.39	....	....	....	8.20	8.33	8.54	....	....	....	....	....	....	....	....	....	....	....	....	....
Rahway	12.40	1.11	2.00	....	5.20	6.40	....	7.06	7.20	7.42	....	8.03	....	....	8.36	8.57	9.10	9.18	9.40	....	10.40	10.53	11.10	11.40	12.10	....	12.40	1.10	1.40
Metro Park (Iselin)	12.44	....	2.04	4.26	5.24	....	6.56	7.10	7.25	....	8.04	8.07	8.15	....	8.40	....	9.14	....	9.44	10.14	10.44	....	11.14	11.44	12.14	....	12.44	1.14	1.44
Metuchen	12.48	....	2.08	....	5.28	....	....	7.14	7.29	....	....	....	....	....	8.44	....	9.18	....	9.48	10.18	10.48	....	11.18	11.48	12.18	....	12.48	1.18	1.48
Edison	12.51	....	2.11	....	....	....	....	7.17	7.32	....	....	8.14	....	....	8.47	....	9.21	....	....	10.21	....	....	11.21	....	12.21	....	....	1.21	....
New Brunswick	12.55	....	2.15	....	5.35	....	7.05	7.21	7.35	....	....	8.18	8.25	....	8.50	....	9.25	....	9.54	10.25	10.54	....	11.25	11.54	12.25	....	12.54	1.25	1.54
Jersey Avenue	1.02	....	2.18	....	....	....	....	....	7.28	....	....	8.21	....	....	....	....	9.28	....	....	10.28	....	....	11.28	....	12.28	....	....	....	....
Princeton Jct. S	....	....	2.31	....	5.50	....	....	7.19	....	7.50	8.34	....	8.41	....	9.05	....	9.41	....	10.09	....	10.41	11.09	....	11.41	12.09	12.41	1.09	1.41	2.09
Trenton, N.J.	....	....	2.42	4.58	6.03	....	....	7.28	....	8.01	....	8.31	8.44	8.52	....	....	9.16	....	9.52	....	10.19	10.52	11.19	11.52	12.19	12.52	1.22	1.52	2.20

A redesign calms the dominating grid, moves the New York departure times to the very top, de-emphasizes less important data, and adds new information. A separating line is formed by tiny leader dots, which read as gray, making a distinction but not a barricade:

am ◐	3701	3301	3801	67	3803	3201	51	3703	3807	3203	61	3809	47	3901	3811	3903	3813	3205	3815	3817	3819	3207	3821	3823	3825
New York, NY	12.10	12.40	1.30	3.52	4.50	6.10	6.25	6.35	6.50	7.10	7.30	7.33	7.45	7.50	8.05	8.25	8.40	8.50	9.10	9.40	10.10	10.25	10.40	11.10	11.40
Newark, NJ[P]	12.24	12.55	1.44	4.07	5.04	6.24	6.38	6.49	7.04	7.24	7.45	7.47	7.59	8.04	8.19	8.39	8.54	9.04	9.24	9.54	10.24	10.39	10.54	11.24	11.54
North Elizabeth										7.30				8.10											
Elizabeth	12.31	1.03	1.51		5.11	6.31		6.56	7.11	7.32		7.54		8.13	8.26	8.46	9.01	9.11	9.31	10.01	10.31	10.46	11.01	11.31	12.01
Linden	12.36		1.56		5.16	6.36		7.01	7.15	7.37		7.59		8.18	8.31	8.51	9.06		9.36	10.06	10.36		11.06	11.36	12.06
North Rahway								7.03		7.39				8.20	8.33	8.54									
Rahway	12.40	1.11	2.00		5.20	6.40		7.06	7.20	7.42		8.03		8.24	8.36	8.57	9.10	9.18	9.40	10.10	10.40	10.53	11.10	11.40	12.10
Metro Park (Iselin)	12.44		2.04	4.26	5.24		6.56	7.10	7.25		8.04	8.07	8.15		8.40		9.14		9.44	10.14	10.44		11.14	11.44	12.14
Metuchen	12.48		2.08		5.28			7.14	7.29			8.11			8.44		9.18		9.48	10.18	10.48		11.18	11.48	12.18
Edison	12.51		2.11					7.17	7.32			8.14			8.47		9.21			10.21			11.21		12.21
New Brunswick	12.55		2.15		5.35		7.05	7.21	7.35			8.18	8.25		8.50		9.25		9.54	10.25	10.54		11.25	11.54	12.25
Jersey Avenue	1.02		2.18					7.28				8.21					9.28			10.28			11.28		12.28
Princeton Junction[S]			2.31		5.50		7.19		7.50			8.34	8.41		9.05		9.41		10.09	10.41	11.09		11.41	12.09	12.41
Trenton, NJ			2.42	4.58	6.03		7.28		8.01		8.31	8.44	8.52		9.16		9.52		10.19	10.52	11.19		11.52	12.19	12.52
NOTES		XM		➤	3	3	➤3	3	3	3	➤3	3	➤3	3	3	3	3								

The focus is now given over to information, transparently organized by an *implicit* typographical grid, defined simply by the absence of type. Nevertheless, data-imprisonment spans centuries of information-design struggles. At right is a touchingly ramshackle grid from a 1535 edition of *Cosmographia*. But, from the virtuoso of typographic design: "Tables should not be set to look like nets with every number enclosed," wrote Jan Tschichold in *Asymmetric Typography*:

> The setting of tables, often approached with gloom, may with careful thought be turned into work of great pleasure. First, try to do without rules altogether. They should be used only when they are absolutely necessary. Vertical rules are needed only when the space between columns is so narrow that mistakes will occur in reading without rules. Tables without vertical rules look better; thin rules are better than thick ones.[2]

Even quite small changes in line can have significant visual effects. For Paul Klee's sketch, the easy and graceful separation of black line and red commentary collapses into a mishmash when color and light/dark differences are minimized:

S.	S.M.	S.M.	S.M.	S.
0	0.0	12.16	20.38	30
1	0.26	12.37	20.40	29
2	0.52	12.58	21.0	28
3	1.18	13.19	21.11	7
4	1.44	13.40	21.31	26
5	2.10	14.0	21.31	25
6	2.36	14.20	21.49	24
7	3.2	14.40	21.49	23
8	3.28	14.50	21.58	22
9	3.53	15.18	22.6	21
10	2.19	15.37	22.14	20
11	4.45	15.55	22.21	19
12	5.10	16.13	22.28	18
13	5.35	16.31	22.35	17
14	6.0	16.48	22.41	16
15	6.25	17.5	22.47	15
16	6.50	17.22	22.52	4
17	7.15	17.38	22.57	1
18	7.39	17.54	23.2	11
19	8.3	18.10	23.7	11
20	8.27	18.5	23.11	10
21	8.51	18.40	23.15	9
22	9.15	18.55	23.18	8
23	9.30	19.9	23.21	7
24	10.2	19.23	23.23	6
25	10.2	19.36	23.25	5
26	10.48	19.49	23.27	4
27	11.10	20.2	23.28	3
28	11.32	20.14	23.29	2
29	11.54	20.26	23.30	1
30	12.16	20.38	23.30	0

[2] Jan Tschichold, *Asymmetric Typography* (Basel, 1935; Toronto, 1967), 62.

Paul Klee, *Symptomatic*. Pen and ink drawing, 1927/F2. From *Das bildnerische Denken* (Basel, 1956), 300.

Separate macro-annotation explains the micro-detail of hospital costs in this 26-day narrative of one person passing through an intensive care unit. The design is transparent to the disturbing information, as a layered polyphony of voices—time sequence, accounting data, commentary—weave together to trace out days, hours, minutes, dollars.

Redrawn from David Hellerstein, "The Slow, Costly Death of Mrs. K_______," *Harper's*, 268 (March 1984), 84–89.

Mrs. K____ has been taken to the emergency room of a renowned hospital on Manhattan's Upper East Side. The doctors "work her up." More than $200 worth of blood tests are ordered ("emer rm lab," "lab serology out"), $232 worth of X-rays taken, $97.50 worth of drugs administered. I never saw Mrs. K____, she wasn't in my hospital, I don't know her medical history. But I am a doctor, and can reconstruct from her hospital bill what is going on, more or less. She is sick, very sick.

Mrs. K____ has been moved to the Intensive Care Unit ("room ICU"). It costs $500 a day to stay in the ICU, base rate. California has the highest average ICU rates in the country: $632 a day. In Mississippi, the average is $265. ICUs were developed in the 1960s. They provide technological life-support systems and allow for extraordinary patient monitoring. An inhalation blood-gas monitor ("inhal blood gas mont") is being used to keep a close check on the amount of oxygen in her blood. Without the attention she is receiving in the ICU, Mrs. K____ might already be dead.

Mrs. K____ has been running a high fever. The doctors have sent cultures of her blood, urine, and sputum to the lab to find out why. She is put on gentamicin ("lab gentamycin troug"), a powerful antibiotic. Such strong drugs can have toxic side effects. Gentamicin kills bacteria, but can also cause kidney failure.

It is Mrs. K____'s fifth day at the hospital, and she is slipping closer to death: her lungs begin to fail. She is put on a respirator ("inhal respirator"), which costs $119 a day to rent and requires a special technician to operate. A hospital can buy the machine for about $15,000.

BILL TO	INSURANCE COVERAGE
JOHN K____	BLUE CROSS STD 21

DATE	DESCRIPTION		TOTAL CHARGES
DETAIL	OF CURRENT CHARGES AND PAYMENTS		
09/23	EMER RM OTHER	5009000	119.00
09/23	EMER RM LAB	5006000	172.00
09/23	LAB SEROLOGY OUT	1406800	35.00
09/23	EMER RM EKG	5007000	61.00
09/23	X-RAY ABDOMEN	1501001	58.00
09/23	X-RAY CHEST RTN	1501009	58.00
09/23	X-RAY CHEST RTN	1501009	58.00
09/23	X-RAY CHEST RTN	1501009	58.00
09/23	PHARMACY	2601000	2.25
09/23	EMER RM PHARMACY	5002000	46.00
09/23	PHARMACY	2601000	49.25
09/23	ROOM ICU		500.00
09/24	LAB AUTO BLOOD CT	1402101	17.00
09/24	LAB ACT PAR THROM	1404001	27.00
09/24	LAB PROTH DETER	1404011	17.00
09/24	LAB BLOOD CULT	1405002	37.00
09/24	LAB BLOOD CULT	1405002	37.00
09/24	LAB CHEM-20	1401104	31.00
09/24	SP HEM CBC	1602010	28.00
09/24	SP HEM RETIC CT	1602046	17.00
09/24	SP HEM PLATELET CT	1602090	17.00
09/24	LAB SEROLOGY OUT	1406800	35.00
09/24	LAB MAGNES	1401042	27.00
09/24	LAB RTN URINAL	1403001	16.00
09/24	LAB RTN CULT	1405003	37.00
09/24	LAB BACTERIA SM	1405011	16.00
09/24	LAB RTN CULT	1405003	37.00
09/24	LAB DIFF	1402099	15.00
09/24	LAB PROT ELEC	1401049	53.00
09/24	LAB FUNGUS	1405008	31.00
09/24	LAB FUNGUS	1405008	31.00
09/24	LAB TBC CULT	1405014	42.00
09/24	LAB DIFF	1402099	15.00
09/24	LAB AUTO BLOOD CT	1402101	17.00
09/24	X-RAY CHEST-BED	1501128	74.00
09/24	PHARMACY	2601000	10.00
09/24	PHARMACY	2601000	8.00
09/24	PHARMACY	2601000	8.00
09/24	PHARMACY	2601000	4.50
09/24	SPECIMEN MUCUS TRAP	2709085	3.00
09/24	SPECIMEN MUCUS TRAP	2709035	3.00
09/24	INHAL BLOOD GAS MONT	2101034	354.00
09/24	ROOM ICU		500.00
09/25	LAB SALICYLATE	1401050	49.00
09/25	LAB AMMONIA	1401006	40.00
09/25	LAB CHEM-20	1401104	31.00
09/25	LAB PROTH DETER	1404011	17.00
09/25	LAB CHEM-8	1401111	31.00
09/25	LAB BACTERIA SM	1405011	16.00
09/25	LAB AUTO BLOOD CT	1402101	17.00
09/25	LAB AUTO BLOOD CT	1402101	17.00
09/25	LAB ACT PAR THROM	1404001	27.00
09/25	LAB TBC CULT	1405014	42.00
09/25	LAB TBC CULT	1405014	42.00
09/25	LAB FUNGUS	1405008	3L.00
09/25	LAB RTN CULT	1405003	37.00
09/25	LAB RTN CULT	1405003	37.00
09/25	CARDIO ROUTINE EKG	1801001	61.00
09/25	X-RAY CHEST-BED	1501128	74.00
09/25	X-RAY ABDOMEN	1501001	58.00
09/25	X-RAY CHEST-BED	1501128	74.00
09/25	X-RAY CHEST-BED	1501128	74.00
09/25	PHARMACY	2601000	13.50
09/25	PHARMACY	2601000	39.00
09/25	PHARMACY	2601000	3.70
09/25	PHARMACY	2601000	16.50
09/25	PHAR IV SOLUTIONS	2601003	16.00
09/25	PHARMACY	2601000	2.50
09/25	PHAR IV SOLUTIONS	2601003	13.50
09/25	PHAR IV SOLUTIONS	2601003	13.50
09/25	PHARMACY	2601000	3.35
09/25	PHARMACY	2601000	2.25
09/25	INHAL BLOOD GAS MONT	2101014	354.00
09/25	ROOM ICU		500.00
09/26	LAB PROTH DETER	1404011	17.00
09/26	LAB CHEM-8	1401111	31.00
09/26	LAB AUTO BLOOD CT	1402101	L7.00
09/26	LAB UR SODIUM	1401077	27.00
09/26	LAB UR POTASS	1401076	27.00
09/26	LAB DIFF	1402099	15.00
09/26	LAB CHEM-8	1401111	31.00
09/26	LAB GENTAMYCIN TROUG	1401112	27.00
09/26	CARDIO ROUTINE EKG	1801001	61.00
09/26	X-RAY CHEST BED	1501128	74.00
09/26	PHARMACY	2601000	31.20
09/26	PHARMACY	2601000	3.70
09/26	PHARMACY	2601000	13.50
09/26	PHARMACY	2601000	39.00
09/27	LAB CHEM-8	1401111	31.00
09/27	LAB PROTH DETER	1404011	17.00
09/27	LAB DIFF	1402099	15.00
09/27	LAB AUTO BLOOD CT	1402101	17.00
09/27	LAB ACT PAR THROM	1404001	27.00
09/27	LAB CHEM-8	1401111	31.00
09/27	LAB CHEM-20	1401104	31.00
09/27	LAB CHEMISTRY OUT	1401800	10.00
09/27	LAB FECES CULT	1405007	40.00
09/27	CARDIO ROUTINE EKG	1801001	61.00
09/27	BLD BK ANTIBDY SCRN	1701004	23.00
09/27	BLD BK ADMIN FEE	1701028	69.00
09/27	PHAR IV SOLUTIONS	2601003	37.50
09/27	PHAR IV SOLUTIONS	2601003	11.00
09/27	PHAR IV SOLUTIONS	2601003	26.00
09/27	PHAR IV SOLUTIONS	2601003	13.50
09/27	PHAR IV SOLUTIONS	2601003	63.50
09/27	PHARMACY	2601000	40.50
09/27	PHARMACY	2601000	11.00
09/27	PHARMACY	2601000	9.00
09/27	PHARMACY	2601000	13.50
09/27	PHARMACY	2601000	39.00
09/27	PHARMACY	2601000	3.70
09/27	PHARMACY	2601000	2.50
09/27	PACK CE 250 PROC FEE	1701018	46.00
09/27	25 NSA 50MU PROC FEE	1701077	35.00
09/27	INFUSION PUMP	2705027	30.00
09/27	INHAL RESPIRATOR	2102015	119.00
09/27	ROOM ICU		500.00
09/28	OPER OP RM 150	1001005	521.00
09/28	LAB OCC BLOOD	1403021	16.00
09/28	LAB GENTAMYCIN TROUG	1401117	27.00
09/28	LAB DIFF	1402079	15.00
09/28	LAB RTN CULT	1405003	37.00
09/28	CARDIO ROUTINE EKG	1801001	61.00
09/28	BLD BK GROUP RH	1701002	28.00
09/28	BLD BK X MATCH	1701006	46.00
09/28	BLD BK ANTIBDY SCRN	1701004	23.00
09/28	X-RAY CHEST-BED	1501128	74.00
09/28	X-RAY CHEST-BED	1501128	74.00
09/28	PHARMACY	2601000	11.00
09/28	PHAR IV SOLUTIONS	2601003	13.50
09/28	PHAR IV SOLUTIONS	2601003	50.00
09/28	PHARMACY	2601000	3.70
09/28	PHARMACY	2601000	39.00
09/28	PHARMACY	2601000	9.00
09/28	PHARMACY	2601000	13.50
09/28	ANEST ANEST DRUGS	1103001	12.40
09/28	INHAL RESPIRATOR	2102015	119.00
09/28	OPER OP RM SUPPLY	1002000	198.00
09/28	SUCT MACHINE-CONT	2704015	22.00
09/28	DIAL SOLN 1.5-CASE	2709040	24.00
09/28	INHAL BLOOD GAS MONT	2101034	354.00
09/29	LAB CHEM-8	1401111	31.00
09/29	LAB CHEM-20	1401104	31.00
09/29	LAB AUTO BLOOD CT	1402101	17.00
09/29	LAB DIFF	1402099	15.00
09/29	LAB DIAG SM/MILL	1407002	40.00
09/29	LAB AUTO BLOOD CT	1402101	17.00
09/29	LAB AUTO BLOOD CT	1402101	17.00
09/29	LAB DIFF	1402099	15.00
09/29	LAB DIFF	1402099	15.00
09/29	LAB GENTAMYCIN TROUG	1401112	27.00
09/29	LAB SP FL CELL CT	1402018	26.00
09/29	LAB CHEM-8	1401111	31.00
09/29	LAB CHEM-8	1401111	31.00
09/29	LAB CHEM-8	1401111	31.00
09/29	LAB FUNGUS	1405008	31.00
09/29	LAB BACTERIOLOGY OUT	1405800	35.00
09/29	LAB OVA & PARASITES	1405018	31.00
09/29	LAB SM&CELL BLOCK	1407003	53.00
09/29	LAB FIBRIN QUAN	1404007	40.00
09/29	LAB COAG FIBRIN SPLT	1404018	49.00
09/29	LAB ACT PAR THROM	1404001	27.00
09/29	LAB AUTO BLOOD CT	1402101	17.00
09/29	LAB FROZEN SECT	1408004	119.00
09/29	LAB RTN CULT	1405003	37.00
09/29	BLD BK COLD AGG	1701007	18.00
09/29	BLD BK ADMIN FEE	1701028	23.00
09/29	X-RAY CHEST-BED	1501128	74.00
09/29	X-RAY ABDOMEN	1501001	58.00
09/29	PHARMACY	2601000	13.50
09/29	PHARMACY	2601000	11.00
09/29	PHAR IV SOLUTIONS	2601003	50.00
09/29	PHARMACY	2601000	39.00
09/29	PHARMACY	2601000	3.70
09/29	ISOLATION GLOVES-BOX	2709025	7.00
09/29	HEEL-ELBOW PROTECTOR	2706025	9.00
09/29	HEEL-ELBOW PROTECTOR	2706025	9.00
09/29	DIAL-PERID KIT 87110	2708015	14.00
09/29	DIAL SOLN 1.5 CASE	2709040	24.00
09/29	SPECIMEN MUCUS TRAP	2709085	3.00
09/29	INHAL BLOOD GAS MONT	2101034	354.00
09/29	INHAL BLOOD GAS MONT	2101034	354.00
09/29	INHAL BLOOD GAS MONT	2101034	354.00
09/29	ROOM ICU		500.00
09/30	LAB AUTO BLOOD CT	1402101	17.00
09/30	LAB CHEM-8	1401111	31.00
09/30	LAB CHEM-8	1401111	31.00
09/30	LAB DIFF	1402099	15.00
09/30	SP HEM COAG STDY COM	1602007	239.00
09/30	SP HEMATOLOGY	1600000	49.00
09/30	SP HEM RETIC CT	1602046	17.00
09/30	SP HEM CBC	1602010	28.00
09/30	LAB BACTERIA SM	1405011	16.00
09/30	LAB ACT PAR THROM	1404001	27.00
09/30	LAB PROTH DETER	1404011	17.00
09/30	LAB FIBRIN QUAN	1404007	40.00
09/30	LAB AUTO BLOOD CT	1402101	17.00
09/30	LAB CHEM-20	1401104	31.00
09/30	LAB TBC CULT	1405014	42.00
09/30	LAB CHEM-20	1401104	31.00
09/30	LAB RTN CULT	1405003	37.00
09/30	LAB RTN CULT	1405003	37.00
09/30	BLD BK ADMIN FEE	1701028	207.00
09/30	X-RAY CHEST-BED	1501128	74.00
09/30	X-RAY CHEST-BED	1501128	74.00
09/30	PHAR IV SOLUTIONS	2601003	16.00
09/30	PHARMACY	2601000	39.00
09/30	PHAR IV SOLUTIONS	2601003	21.00
09/30	PHAR IV SOLUTIONS	2601003	16.00
09/30	PHARMACY	2601000	3.70
09/30	PHARMACY	2601000	13.50
09/30	PHARMACY	2601000	11.00
09/30	PHARMACY	2601000	2.25
09/30	PHAR IV SOLUTIONS	2601000	21.00
09/30	PHAR IV SOLUTIONS	2601000	21.00
09/30	PHAR IV SOLUTIONS	2601003	18.50
09/30	PHARMACY	2601000	2.50
09/30	PLAT CONC PROC FEE	1701014	180.00
09/30	FRSH FR PLA PROC FEE	1701019	26.00
09/30	INHAL RESPIRATOR	2102015	119.00
09/30	DRESSING SET-DISP.	2708041	7.00
09/30	VEST RESTRAINT	2709032	12.00
09/30	INHAL BLOOD GAS MONT	2101034	354.00
09/30	ROOM ICU		500.00
10/01	LAB CHEM-20	1401104	31.00
10/01	LAB CHEM-8	1401111	31.00
10/01	LAB CHEM-8	1401111	31.00
10/01	LAB CHEM-8	1401111	31.00
10/01	LAB DIFF	1402099	15.00
10/01	LAB AUTO BLOOD CT	1402101	17.00
10/01	BLD BK ADMIN FEE	1701028	23.00
10/01	X-RAY CHEST-BED	1501128	74.00
10/01	PHAR IV SOLUTIONS	2601003	37.50
10/01	PHARMACY	2601000	13.50
10/01	PHARMACY	2601000	11.00
10/01	PHARMACY	2601000	3.70
10/01	PHARMACY	2601000	31.20
10/01	PHARMACY	2601000	2.40
10/01	PHARMACY	2601000	27.20
10/01	PHAR IV SOLUTIONS	2601003	13.50
10/01	25 NSA 50MU PROC FEE	1701077	35.00
10/01	INHAL RESPIRATOR	2102015	119.00
10/02	PHARMACY	2601000	27.20

Mrs. K____'s first week in Intensive Care ends in a flourish of blood tests. She has five Chem-8s ("lab chem-8")—tests that measure the levels of sodium, potassium, and six other chemicals in her blood. The hospital charges Mrs. K____ $31 for each Chem-8. Most independent labs charge about half as much; some hospitals charge up to $60. The *New England Journal of Medicine* has said: "The clinical laboratory [is] a convenient profit center that can be used to support unrelated deficit-producing hospital operations." The *Annals of Internal Medicine* estimates that the number of clinical lab tests being done is rising 15 percent a year.

Mrs. K____ has started peritoneal dialysis ("dial-perid kit 87110"). Her kidneys are failing. She is still hooked up to the respirator. She is being kept alive by what Lewis Thomas calls "halfway technologies" — "halfway" because kidney dialysis machines and respirators can support organ systems for long periods of time, but can't cure the underlying disease. Some doctors are beginning to question this practice. A recent study at the George Washington University Medical Center concluded: "Substantial medical resources are now being used in aggressive but frequently futile attempts to avoid death."

Mrs. K____ has been put in a vest restraint. Restraints are used in Intensive Care to keep patients from thrashing about or pulling their tubes out. Many ICU patients develop what is called "ICU psychosis." They become disoriented, begin hallucinating. The condition is brought on by lack of sleep, toxic drugs, the noise of the ICU staff and machines, and pain.

Mrs. K ____ has been on the respirator for six days. It is breathing for her. But there has been a problem. The tube running from the machine into her mouth and down her throat was not bringing enough oxygen to her lungs. She needed a tracheotomy ("trach care set"). The tube from the respirator is now attached directly to her trachea, through a hole cut into her neck.

This charge—for a blood product ("5 NSA 250MU proc fee") —is not covered by Mrs. K ____ 's Blue Cross policy. The policy also does not cover the cost of fresh blood plasma ("frsh fr pla proc fee"). These charges have been mounting. Mrs. K ____ is bleeding internally.

Mrs. K ____ has been in Intensive Care for two weeks. She is still running a very high fever. The doctors are still testing. Mrs. K ____ has been placed on a special blanket; it is hooked up to a machine that functions like a refrigerator ("hypothermia machine"). The machine cools the blanket, and the blanket helps lower Mrs. K ____ 's body temperature. Should her temperature rise too high, she may suffer permanent brain damage.

Mrs. K ____ has undergone a gated blood-pool study ("nuc med sec/pool sty"). The doctors have "tagged" her red blood cells with a radioactive isotope. Using a camera that picks up the isotope, the doctors can watch the passage of blood through her heart. In this way, they see firsthand whether the ventricles are functioning properly—whether enough blood is getting pumped, enough oxygen is being sent through the body. First her lungs, then her kidneys. Now Mrs. K ____ 's heart seems to be going.

10/02	PHARMACY	2601000	27.20
10/02	PHARMACY	2601000	2.40
10/02	PHARMACY	2601000	2.50
10/02	PHARMACY	2601000	2.25
10/02	FRSH FR PLA PROC FEE	1701019	26.00
10/02	TRACH CARE SET	2705009	3.00
10/02	TRACH CARE SET	2705009	3.00
10/02	TRACH CARE SET	2705009	3.00
10/02	TRACH CARE SET	2705009	3.00
10/03	INHAL BLOOD GAS MONT	2101034	354.00
10/03	ROOM ICU		500.00
10/04	LAB CHEM-8	1401111	31.00
10/04	LAB AUTO BLOOD CT	1402101	17.00
10/04	LAB PROTH DETER	1404011	17.00
10/04	LAB DIFF	1402099	15.00
10/04	LAB ACT PAR THROM	1404001	27.00
10/04	LAB RTN URINAL	1403001	16.00
10/04	LAB RTN CULT	1405003	37.00
10/04	BLD BK ADMIN FEE	1701028	69.00
10/04	X-RAY CHEST-BED	1501128	74.00
10/04	PHAR IV SOLUTIONS	2601003	16.00
10/04	PHAR IV SOLUTIONS	2601003	11.00
10/04	PHAR IV SOLUTIONS	2601003	18.50
10/04	PHAR IV SOLUTIONS	2601003	21.00
10/04	PHARMACY	2601000	55.50
10/04	PHARMACY	2601000	31.20
10/04	PHARMACY	2601000	2.40
10/04	PHARMACY	2601000	5.00
10/04	25 NSA 50MU PROC FEE	1701077	35.00
10/04	FRSH FR PLA PROC FEE	1701019	52.00
10/04	INHAL BLOOD GAS MONT	2101034	354.00
10/04	ROOM ICU		500.00
10/05	LAB AUTO BLOOD CT	1402101	17.00
10/05	LAB DIFF	1402099	15.00
10/05	LAB CHEM-8	1401111	31.00
10/05	LAB CHEM-20	1401104	31.00
10/05	LAB CORTISOL	1401021	27.00
10/05	LAB CORTISOL	1401021	27.00
10/05	LAB RTN CULT	1405003	37.00
10/05	LAB ACT PAR THROM	1404001	27.00
10/05	LAB PROTH DETER	1404011	17.00
10/05	BLD BK ADMIN FEE	1701028	46.00
10/05	X-RAY CHEST-BED	1501128	74.00
10/05	XRAY SONOGRAM	1505012	117.00
10/05	PHAR IV SOLUTIONS	2601003	23.50
10/05	PHARMACY	2601000	2.40
10/05	PHARMACY	2601000	31.20
10/05	PHARMACY	2601000	55.50
10/05	PHARMACY	2601000	2.40
10/05	PHAR IV SOLUTIONS	2601003	50.00
10/05	PHARMACY	2601000	96.00
10/05	PHARMACY	2601000	15.00
10/05	5 NSA 250MU PROC FEE	1701074	35.00
10/05	25 NSA 50MU PROC FEE	1701077	35.00
10/05	DIALYSIS CART	2704008	70.00
10/05	INHAL BLOOD GAS MONT	2101034	354.00
10/05	ROOM ICU		500.00
10/06	LAB CHEM-20	1401104	31.00
10/06	LAB ACT PAR THROM	1404001	27.00
10/06	LAB PROTH DETER	1404011	17.00
10/06	LAB DIFF	1402099	15.00
10/06	LAB AUTO BLOOD CT	1402101	17.00
10/06	LAB CHEM-8	1401111	31.00
10/06	LAB CHEM-20	1401104	31.00
10/06	LAB BLOOD CULT	1405002	37.00
10/06	LAB BLOOD CULT	1405002	37.00
10/06	LAB PROTH DETER	1404011	17.00
10/06	LAB ACT PAR THROM	1404001	27.00
10/06	BLD BK ADMIN FEE	1701028	23.00
10/06	X-RAY CHEST-BED	1501128	74.00
10/06	X-RAY CHEST-BED	1501128	74.00
10/06	PHAR IV SOLUTIONS	2601003	26.00
10/06	PHARMACY	2601000	2.40
10/06	PHARMACY	2601000	55.50
10/06	PHARMACY	2601000	31.20
10/06	PHAR IV SOLUTIONS	2601003	99.00
10/06	PHARMACY	2601000	249.60
10/06	PHAR IV SOLUTIONS	2601003	13.50
10/06	PHAR IV SOLUTIONS	2601003	37.50
10/06	PHARMACY	2601000	2.40
10/06	25 NSA 50MU PROC FEE	1701077	35.00
10/06	INFUSION PUMP	2705027	30.00
10/06	DIAL SOLN 1.5-CASE	2709040	24.00
10/06	HYPOTHERMIA MACHINE	2704006	25.00
10/06	ROOM ICU		500.00
10/07	LAB ACT PAR THROM	1404001	27.00
10/07	LAB PROTH DETER	1404011	17.00
10/07	LAB AUTO BLOOD CT	1402101	17.00
10/07	LAB DIFF	1402099	15.00
10/07	LAB CHEM-8	1401111	31.00
10/07	LAB CHEM-8	1401111	31.00
10/07	LAB CHEM-20	1401104	31.00
10/07	LAB CHEM-8	1401111	31.00
10/07	LAB CHEM-20	1401104	31.00
10/07	LAB CHEM-8	1401111	31.00
10/08	PHARMACY	2601000	55.50
10/08	PHARMACY	2601000	31.20
10/08	PHAR IV SOLUTIONS	2601003	18.50
10/08	PHARMACY	2601000	5.00
10/08	PHARMACY	2601000	5.00
10/08	PHARMACY	2601000	5.00
10/08	PHARMACY	2601000	62.00
10/08	INHAL RESPIRATOR	2102015	119.00
10/08	ISOLATION GLOVES-BOX	2709025	7.00
10/08	DIAL SOLN 1.5-CASE	2709040	24.00
10/08	INHAL BLOOD GAS MONT	2101034	354.00
10/08	ROOM ICU		500.00
10/09	LAB ACT PAR THROM	1404001	27.00
10/09	LAB PROTH DETER	1404011	17.00
10/10	LAB ACT PAR THROM	1404001	27.00
10/10	CARDIO ROUTINE EKG	1801001	61.00
10/10	X-RAY CHEST-BED	1501128	74.00
10/11	LAB CHEM-8	1401111	31.00
10/11	LAB CHEM-8	1401111	31.00
10/11	ROOM ICU		500.00
10/12	PHAR IV SOLUTIONS	2601003	37.50
10/12	PHARMACY	2601000	2.40
10/12	25 NSA 50MU PROC FEE	1701077	70.00
10/12	INHAL RESPIRATOR	2101015	119.00
10/12	INHAL RESPIRATOR	2102015	119.00
10/12	DIAL SOLN 1.5-CASE	2709040	24.00
10/12	PLASTIC TRACH TUBE	2705007	26.00
10/12	PLASTIC TRACH TUBE	2705007	26.00
10/12	DIALYSIS CART	2704008	70.00
10/12	INHAL BLOOD GAS MONT	2101034	354.00
10/12	ROOM ICU		500.00
10/13	LAB DIFF	1402099	15.00
10/13	LAB AUTO BLOOD CT	1402101	17.00
10/13	LAB PROTH DETER	1404011	17.00
10/13	LAB ACT PAR THROM	1404001	27.00
10/13	LAB CHEM-20	1401104	31.00
10/13	LAB CHEM-8	1401111	31.00
10/13	LAB CHEM-8	1401111	31.00
10/13	LAB CHEM-8	1401111	31.00
10/13	LAB CHEM-8	1401111	31.00
10/13	LAB DIFF	1402099	15.00
10/13	LAB RTN CULT	1405003	37.00
10/13	LAB AUTO BLOOD CT	1402101	17.00
10/13	LAB BACTERIA SM	1405011	16.00
10/13	LAB RTN CULT	1405003	37.00
10/13	LAB RTN CULT	1405003	37.00
10/13	NUC MED SEC/POOL STY	3001021	170.00
10/13	BLD BK ADMIN FEE	1701028	23.00
10/13	BLD BK ANTIBDY SCRN	1701004	23.00
10/13	BLD BK DIR COOMBS	1701031	18.00
10/13	X-RAY CHEST-BED	1501128	74.00
10/13	PHARMACY	2601000	2.40
10/13	PHAR IV SOLUTIONS	2601003	26.00
10/13	PHAR IV SOLUTIONS	2601003	26.00
10/13	PHARMACY	2601000	31.20
10/13	PHARMACY	2601000	55.50
10/13	PHARMACY	2601000	14.50
10/13	PHARMACY	2601000	2.40
10/13	PHAR IV SOLUTIONS	2601003	21.00
10/14	PACK CE 250 PROC FEE	1701013	92.00
10/14	25 NSA 50MU PROC FEE	1701077	35.00
10/14	INHAL RESPIRATOR	2102015	119.00
10/14	INHAL BLOOD GAS MONT	2101034	354.00
10/14	ROOM ICU		500.00
10/15	LAB CHEM-8	1401111	31.00
10/15	LAB CHEM-8	1401111	31.00
10/15	LAB CHEM-20	1401104	31.00
10/15	LAB INDIA INK	1405009	17.00
10/15	LAB FUNGUS	1405008	31.00
10/15	LAB TBC CULT	1405014	42.00
10/15	LAB HETER MONO	1406005	25.00
10/15	LAB UR ELECTROPHORES	1403007	26.00
10/15	LAB CHEM-8	1401111	31.00
10/15	LAB CHEM-8	1401111	31.00
10/15	LAB SP FL CELL CT	1402018	26.00
10/15	LAB CHEM-8	1401111	31.00
10/15	LAB SP FL GLUC	1401056	27.00
10/15	LAB SP FL PROT	1401057	27.00
10/15	LAB MAGNES	1401042	27.00
10/15	LAB TOT BILI	1401008	28.00
10/16	LAB CHEM-8	1401111	31.00
10/16	LAB CHEM-8	1401111	31.00
10/16	LAB AUTO BLOOD CT	1402101	17.00
10/16	LAB RTN CULT	1405003	37.00
10/16	LAB ANTIBIOT SENS	1405001	40.00
10/16	LAB BACTERIA SM	1405011	16.00
10/16	X-RAY CHEST-BED	1501128	74.00
10/16	PHAR IV SOLUTIONS	2601003	13.50
10/16	PHARMACY	2601000	14.50
10/16	PHARMACY	2601000	2.40
10/16	PHARMACY	2601000	31.20
10/16	PHARMACY	2601000	2.40
10/16	PHARMACY	2601000	2.40
10/16	PHARMACY	2601000	24.00
10/16	PHARMACY	2601000	297.00
10/16	INHAL RESPIRATOR	2102015	119.00
10/16	HYPOTHERMIA MACHINE	2704006	25.00
10/16	ISOLATION GLOVES-BOX	2709025	7.00
10/16	ISOLATION GLOVES-BOX	2709025	7.00
10/16	INHAL BLOOD GAS MONT	2101034	354.00
10/16	ROOM ICU		500.00
10/17	TELEPHONE CHARGE	0000002	48.00
10/17	LAB ACT PAR THROM	1404001	27.00
10/17	LAB CHEM-8	1401111	31.00
10/17	LAB CHEM-8	1401111	31.00
10/17	LAB CHEM-20	1401104	31.00
10/17	LAB CHEM-8	1401111	31.00
10/17	LAB PROTH DETER	1404011	17.00
10/17	LAB CHEM-20	1401104	31.00
10/17	X-RAY CHEST-BED	1501128	74.00
10/17	PHARMACY	2601000	55.50
10/17	PHARMACY	2601000	31.20
10/17	PHARMACY	2601000	2.40
10/17	PHARMACY	2601000	25.00
10/17	PHARMACY	2601000	2.40
10/17	PHARMACY	2601000	2.40
10/17	PHARMACY	2601000	14.50
10/17	PHARMACY	2601000	.80
10/17	PHARMACY	2601000	2.25
10/17	PHARMACY	2601000	2.40
10/17	PHAR IV SOLUTIONS	2601003	13.50
10/17	PHAR IV SOLUTIONS	2601003	37.50
10/17	PHAR IV SOLUTIONS	2601003	16.00
10/17	PHAR IV SOLUTIONS	2601003	21.00
10/17	PHAR IV SOLUTIONS	2601003	13.50
10/17	PHAR IV SOLUTIONS	2601003	16.00
10/17	PHAR IV SOLUTIONS	2601003	16.00
10/17	PHAR IV SOLUTIONS	2601003	16.00
10/17	PHAR IV SOLUTIONS	2601003	50.00
10/17	PHAR IV SOLUTIONS	2601003	37.50
10/17	PHAR IV SOLUTIONS	2601003	37.50
10/17	PHAR IV SOLUTIONS	2601003	37.50
10/17	PHAR IV SOLUTIONS	2601003	16.00
10/18	PLAT CONC PROC FEE	1701014	117.50
10/18	25 NSA 50MU PROC FEE	1701077	35.00
10/18	INHAL RESPIRATOR	2102015	119.00
10/18	INHAL BLOOD GASES	2101006	119.00
10/18	INHAL BLOOD GASES	2101006	119.00

SUMMARY OF CHARGES

OPERATING ROOM	521.00
DRUGS	6364.70
BLOOD SERV & FRACT	1389.50
LABORATORY	11201.00
X-RAY	2870.00
SUPPLIES	3698.00
EKG, EEG, ETC.	366.00
THERAPY	8734.00
MICS NON COVERED	167.00
R&C IN.CARE 24 DAYS 500.00/DAY	12000.00
SUB-TOTAL OF CHARGES	47311.20

TOTAL 47311.20

Mrs. K ____ 's fourth week in the hospital begins with a spinal tap. Using a long needle, a doctor drains fluid from her spinal cord. The fluid is sent to the lab for about a dozen tests ("lab sp fl cell ct"). A spinal tap is performed when a patient has what are called "neurological signs." Partial paralysis is one such sign, loss of consciousness another. When doctors order a spinal tap, they suspect brain disease.

Weeks of halfway technology have given the doctors time for testing. The doctors may even have diagnosed what is wrong with Mrs. K ____ ; it is hard to say. But the ICU and its technology have not given them the ability to cure her. Now the heart, which has been failing, gives out. Cardiac arrest. There is a burst of activity. Bicarbonate, epinephrine, and other drugs ("pharmacy") are administered. Thirteen bottles of intravenous solution ("phar iv solutions") are poured in.

Mrs. K ____ 's last minutes are recorded on the various ICU monitors. The level of oxygen in her blood falls. She dies.

Mrs. K ____ 's bottom line. Total cost of twenty-six days in the hospital, nearly all this time in Intensive Care: $47,311.20. Of this, Blue Cross will pay $41,933.87. The doctors' bills, not covered by hospitalization insurance, probably come to thousands of dollars more. Perhaps Mrs. K ____ had Blue Shield, which covers doctors' fees. In 1982, the last year for which figures are available, Americans spent $322 billion on health care. Of this, $135.5 billion was spent on hospital care. There were 56,241 ICU beds in 1982 like the one Mrs. K ____ was kept alive in, and about $27 billion was spent for their use. That represented nearly one percent of the gross national product.

All elements in the map at right—contours, rivers, roads, names—are at the same visual level with equal values, equal texture, equal color, and even nearly equal shape. An undifferentiated, unlayered surface results, jumbled up, blurry, incoherent, chaotic with unintentional optical art. What we have here is a failure to communicate.

Far more detailed than the perfect jumble, this map below separates and layers information by means of distinctions in shape, value (light to dark), size, and especially color. The negative areas are also informative;

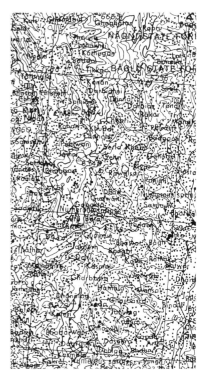

Simla, India (U.S. Army map series U 502, NH 43-4, 1954), based on the Survey of India, 1921–1943.

Tokyo Prefecture. Musashino, Uneo Park, Kurumazaka area (Tokyo, 1884).

light strips formed by the grid of buildings identify roads and paths. The water symbol is a blue field, further differentiated from other color fields by a gentle fading away from each outlined edge. Shown against a dull background rather than bright white, these colors remain both calm and distinctive, avoiding clutter. The map exemplifies the "first rule of color composition" of the illustrious Swiss cartographer, Eduard Imhof:

> Pure, bright or very strong colors have loud, unbearable effects when they stand unrelieved over large areas adjacent to each other, but extraordinary effects can be achieved when they are used sparingly on or between dull background tones. "Noise is not music . . . only on a quiet background can a colorful theme be constructed," claims Windisch.[3]

[3] Eduard Imhof, *Cartographic Relief Presentation* (Berlin, 1982), edited and translated by H. J. Steward from Imhof's *Kartographische Geländedarstellung* (Berlin, 1965), 72. The internal quotation is from H. Windisch, *Schule der Farbenphotographie* (Seebruck, 6th edition, 1958).

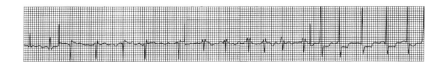

Signal and background compete above, as electrocardiogram trace line becomes caught up in a thick grid. Below, the screened-down grid stays behind traces from each of 12 monitoring leads:[4]

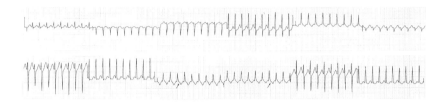

Similarly for music notation, some staff paper is better than others:

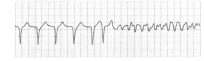

[4] The preferred example is redrawn from J. Marcus Wharton and Nora Goldschlager, *Interpreting Cardiac Dysrhythmias* (Oradell, New Jersey, 1987), 123. Color also layers, as a gray grid calibrates this signal of ventricular fibrillation, a final collapse of the

heart, with only a disorganized rhythm remaining. A similar trace can result from recording artifacts such as a loose monitoring wire; however, one textbook dryly notes, "As the patient will usually have lost consciousness by the time you have realized that it is not just due to a loose connection, diagnosis is easy." John R. Hampton, *The ECG Made Easy* (Edinburgh, 1986), 66.

In Stravinsky's sketchbook for *Sacre du printemps*, a grid quietly but clearly and precisely locates the music. Gray grids almost always work well and, with a delicate line, may promote more accurate data reading

and reconstruction than a heavy grid. Dark grid lines are chartjunk. When a graphic serves as a look-up table (rare indeed), then a grid may help with reading and interpolation. But even then the grid should be muted relative to the data. Often ready-made graph paper comes with darkly printed lines. The reverse unprinted side should be used, for then lines show through faintly and do not clutter the data. If the paper is heavily gridded on both sides, throw it out.

Igor Strawinsky, *Sacre-Skizzenbuch*, 135, top; Paul Sacher Stiftung, Kunstmuseum Basel, and in Hans Oesch, "Im Schatten des *Sacre du printemps* Beobachtungen zu den Trois poésies de la lyrique japonaise, einem Schlüsselwerk von Igor Strawinsky," *Komponisten des 20.Jahrhunderts in der Paul Sacher Stiftung* (Basel, 1986), 100.

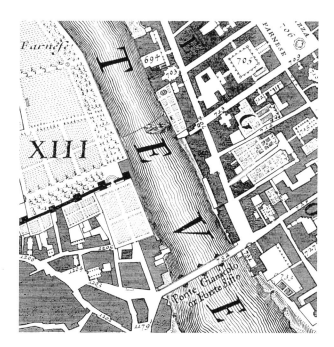

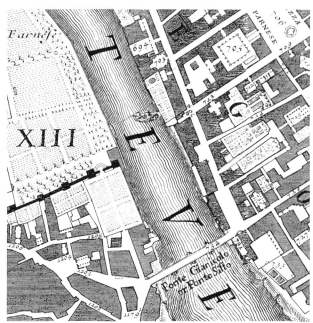

In the masterly 1748 Nolli map of Rome, the river's heavy inking activates what should be a visually tranquil area, causing bridge names and a little boat to vibrate in a moiré prison, albeit a quiet one. Muting the river encoding calms vibration and brings names and other details forward, while retaining a symbolism of rippling water.[5] This redesign and others that we have seen are visual equivalents of Italo Calvino's approach to writing:

> My working method has more often than not involved the subtraction of weight. I have tried to remove weight, sometimes from people, sometimes from heavenly bodies, sometimes from cities; above all I have tried to remove weight from the structure of stories and from language. . . . Maybe I was only then becoming aware of the weight, the inertia, the opacity of the world—qualities that stick to writing from the start, unless one finds some way of evading them.[6]

Layering of data, often achieved by felicitous subtraction of weight, enhances representation of both data dimensionality and density on flatland. Usually this involves creating a hierarchy of visual effects, possibly matching an ordering of information content. Small, modest design moves can yield decisive visual results, as in these intriguing demonstrations of the illusory borders of subjective contours:

[5] Giambattista Nolli, *Pianta Grande di Roma* (Rome, 1748; from a facsimile edition by J. H. Aronson, Highmount, New York, 1984). Note the seemingly English word "or" in the names under the bridge, a result of the 18th-century custom of contracting the Italian *ora*, meaning *now, at this time, currently*. On his map, Nolli cites first the old name *Ponte Gianicolo or[a] Ponte Sisto* (the bridge's new name). Ironically, the English "or" works in this context, although the meaning is not quite right. See Barbara Reynolds, *The Cambridge Italian Dictionary, Italian-English* (Cambridge, 1962), 521.

[6] Italo Calvino, *Six Memos for the Next Millennium* (Cambridge, 1988), 3-4.

Gaetano Kanizsa, "Contours without Gradients or Cognitive Contours?" *Italian Journal of Psychology*, 1 (April 1974), 93-112; and Gaetano Kanizsa, "Subjective Contours," *Scientific American*, 234 (April 1976), 48-52.

Visual activation of negative areas of white space in these exhibits illustrates *the endlessly contextual and interactive nature of visual elements.* This idea is captured in a fundamental principle of information design: *1 + 1 = 3 or more.* In the simplest case, when we draw two black lines, a third visual activity results, a bright white path between the lines (note that this path appears even to have an angled end). And a complexity

of marks generates an exponential complexity of negative shapes. *Most of the time, that surplus visual activity is non-information, noise, and clutter.*[7] This two-step logic—recognition of 1 + 1 = 3 effects and the consideration that they generate noise—provides a valuable guide for refining and editing designs, for graphical reasoning, for subtraction of weight.[8]

In a little-known essay on 1 + 1 = 3 effects, Josef Albers conducts the demonstrations below, a visually sensitive and artistic approach to the cognitive contours of perceptual psychologists. Albers, seeing area and surface rather than border and edge, escapes the preoccupying magic of optical illusions to conceive a broad idea of negative space activation:

Keith Haring, Untitled 4/29/82, sumi ink on paper. © 1992 Estate of Keith Haring.

[7] Rare exceptions are the Turgot-Bretez map of Paris and the Nolli map of Rome: streets, absent of ink, are defined—tersely, clearly, and precisely—by the surrounding ink of blocks and buildings, creating subjective contours.

[8] Note the additional 1 + 1 = 3 effects, on this page, as the interaction between the examples and the surrounding type enlivens the white space, forming shapes, profiles, and paths. These reverberations are vivid because our examples are printed in black; strong light/dark contrasts accentuate the clutter of 1 + 1 = 3 or more.

Here I have 2 equal strips of cardboard (1″ x 6″)

Here is one (vertical), here another (also vertical). Seeing one strip plus one strip, we count 2 strips: 1 + 1 = 2.

We recognize the equal width of the strips. Now, 1 width + 1 width (strips touching) equals 2 widths: 1 + 1 = 2.

But now, separating them (both remain vertical) by 1 width — we count 3 widths (one of them negative) : 1 + 1 = 3.

Of the 2 vertical strips, one crosses the other horizontally in their centers. Result : 2 lines form a crossing thus producing 4 arms, as 4 extensions, to be read inward as well as outward. We also see 4 rectangles, and with some imagination, 4 triangles, 4 squares. By shifting centers and angles, arms and the in-between figures become unequal.

All together : one line plus one line results in many meanings — *Quod erat demonstrandum.*

Josef Albers, "One Plus One Equals Three or More: Factual Facts and Actual Facts," in Albers, *Search Versus Re-Search* (Hartford, 1969), 17-18.

Stumbling over $1 + 1 = 3$ has produced perhaps the worst index ever designed, a rare perfect failure. The preface to this guide for flying small aircraft says, "This manual is primarily intended for use during actual flight instruction." Imagine now noisy vibration in a plane as we search through this visually vibrating list, looking for, say, an entry on "forced landing" . . . and the index turns out to have no page numbers. Only a small segment of the unbearable original is shown.

The noise of $1 + 1 = 3$ is directly proportional to the contrast in value (light/dark) between figure and ground. On white backgrounds, therefore, a varying range of lighter colors will minimize incidental clutter. Three maps at right show these tactics in action. In the first, the bold shapes promote vibration all over; and with only nameless streets down on paper, this map is already in visual trouble. At center, thinning two sides of each block results in every street bordered by one thick *and* one thin line, thus deflecting $1 + 1 = 3$ effects (the thin lines, like gray lines, are *visually* light in value). On the bottom map, gray establishes serene, motionless edges—an arrangement that will easily accommodate additional geographic detail.

Careful visual editing diminishes $1 + 1 = 3$ clutter. These are not trivial cosmetic matters, for signal enhancement through noise reduction can reduce viewer fatigue as well as improve accuracy of readings from a computer interface, a flight-control display, or a medical instrument. Clarity is not everything, but there is little without it. Editing this statistical graph (showing variability about local averages) remedies the visual clutter induced by parallel lines and equal-width white bands. The redesign, at far right, sweeps the noise away, with color spots now smartly tracking the path of averages.

Harmonizing text and line-drawing requires sensitive appraisals of prolific interaction effects. Unless deliberate obscurity is sought, avoid surrounding words by little boxes, which activate negative white spaces

SURGEON GENERAL'S WARNING: SMOKING CAUSES LUNG CANCER, HEART DISEASE, EMPHYSEMA, AND MAY COMPLICATE PREGNANCY

between word and box. And below, the first three maps place the type poorly, with an awkward white stripe materializing between name and river. Type from above adjusts to graphics better, in part because most words have fewer descenders than ascenders (in map 3, a diverting white shape is formed by the ascending letters).[9] These small local details will promptly accumulate on the entire map surface, deciding quality.

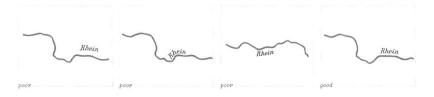

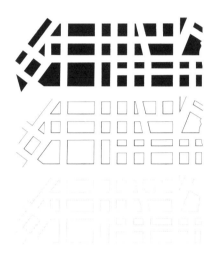

Middle map above, student project by Jon Wertheimer, Studies in Graphic Design, Yale University, 1985-1986.

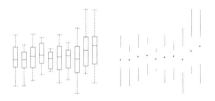

John W. Tukey, *Exploratory Data Analysis* (Reading, Massachusetts, 1977), 269; and, right, Edward R. Tufte, *The Visual Display of Quantitative Information* (Cheshire, Connecticut, 1983), 125.

[9] Eduard Imhof, "Die Anordnung der Namen in der Karte," *International Yearbook of Cartography*, 2 (1962), 93-129; and, in English translation, "Positioning Names on Maps," *The American Cartographer*, 2 (1975), 128-144; showing here 4 of Imhof's total of 106 examples! Also, Paul Bühler, "Schriftformen und Schrifterstellung unter besonderer Berücksichtigung der schweizerischen topographischen Kartenwerke," *International Yearbook of Cartography*, 1 (1961), 153-181.

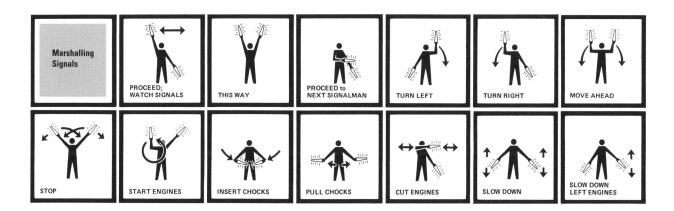

This array above, an information prison, employs a narrow range of strong shapes. Grid, silhouette, and type compete at the same nervous visual level. Too loud and too similar. Thick bars of grid boxes generate little paths around both type and silhouette by exciting the negative white space: 1 + 1 = 3, all over again. Why should the trivial task of dividing up the already free-standing elements become the dominant statement of the entire display?

To direct attention toward the information at hand, the revision below extends the light to dark range of color, separating and layering the data in rough proportion to their relevance. Gray calms a contrasty silhouette, bringing about in turn more emphasis on the lamps and their position and motion. Coloring these lights helps to separate the signals from all the rest. Some 260 lamp-whiskers were erased, whiskers which originally read in confusion as glowing light and also trembling motion. Note the effectiveness and elegance of *small spots of intense, saturated color* for carrying information—a design secret of classical cartography[10] and, for that matter, of traffic lights. Finally, in our revised version, the type for the title (upper left corner) has emerged from its foggy closet. Also the labels, now set in Gill Sans, are no longer equal in visual weight to the motion arrows, among several typographical refinements.

[10] "If one limits strong, heavy, rich, and solid colors to the small areas of extremes, then expressive and beautiful colored area patterns occur. . . . Large area background or base-colors do their work most quietly, allowing the smaller, bright areas to stand out most vividly, if the former are muted, grayish or neutral." Eduard Imhof, *Cartographic Relief Presentation* (Berlin, 1982), edited and translated by H. J. Steward from Imhof's *Kartographische Geländedarstellung* (Berlin, 1965), 72. On visual issues and map-making, see essays by Samuel Y. Edgerton, Jr., Svetlana Alpers, Juergen Schultz, Ulla Ehrensvärd, James A. Welu, and David Woodward, in Woodward, ed., *Art and Cartography* (Chicago, 1987).

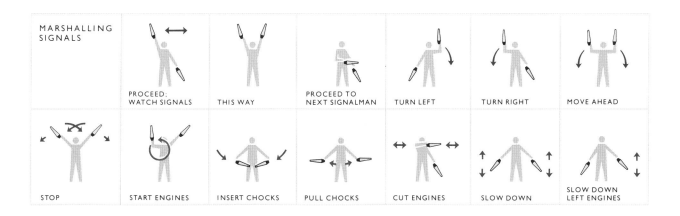

In the statistical graphic at top, the visually most active elements are, of all things, glowing optical white dots that appear at each intersection of grid lines. (The arrangement of many computer interfaces is similarly overwrought.) The doubled-up, tremor-inducing lines consume 18 percent of this technically ingenious chart, a multi-window plot. Here the redrawing, in ungrid style, eliminates the visual noise, concentrating our viewer's attention on data rather than data containers.

Too often epidemics of data-imprisonment and decorative gridding break out when contemporary commercial designers are faced with information. The aggressive visual presence of stylized grids, little boxes surrounding words here and there, and cadenced accents—all so empty of content, irrelevant—becomes the only way you can tell if something has been "designed". At any rate, the self-important grid is for the birds, providing only a nice place to perch:

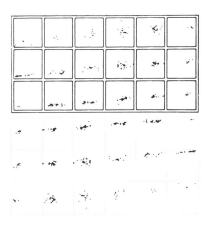

Paul A. Tukey and John W. Tukey, "Data-Driven View Selection: Agglomeration and Sharpening," in Vic Barnett, ed., *Interpreting Multivariate Data* (Chichester, England, 1981), 231–232; and Edward R. Tufte, *The Visual Display of Quantitative Information* (Cheshire, Connecticut, 1983), 114.

Dioscorides (Constantinopolitanus), De materia medica, 6th century, ca 512 A.D., fol. 483. Illumination on vellum, Vienna österreichische Nationalbibliothek, Cod. Med. Gr. 1.

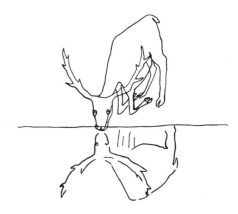

Information consists of *differences that make a difference*. A fruitful method for the enforcement of such differences is to layer and separate data, much as is done on a high-density map. In representing various layers of meaning and reading, the most economical of means can yield distinctions that make a difference: the small gestures of Calder's pen easily separate the stag and his watery reflection. Failure to differentiate among layers of reading leads to cluttered and incoherent displays filled with disinformation, generated by the unrelenting interactive visual arithmetic of flatland, 1 + 1 = 3 or more.

All these ideas—figure and ground, interaction effects, 1 + 1 = 3 or more, layering and separation—have compelling consequences for information displays. Such concepts (operating under an assortment of names) are thoroughly tested, long familiar the world over in the flatlands of typographers, calligraphers, graphic designers, illustrators, artists, and, in three dimensions, architects:

> In every clear concept of the nature of vision and in every healthy approach to the spatial world, this dynamic unity of figure and background has been clearly understood. Lao Tse showed such grasp when he said: "A vessel is useful only through its emptiness. It is the space opened in a wall that serves as a window. Thus it is the nonexistent in things which makes them serviceable." Eastern visual culture has a deep understanding of the role of empty space in the image. Chinese and Japanese painters have the admirable courage to leave empty large paths of their picture-surface so that the surface is divided into unequal intervals which, through their spacing, force the eye of the spectator to movements of varying velocity in following up relationships, and thus create the unity by the greatest possible variation of surface. Chinese and Japanese calligraphy also have a sound respect for the white interval. Characters are written in imaginary squares, the blank areas of which are given as much consideration as the graphic units, the strokes. Written or printed communications are living or dead depending upon the organization of their blank spaces. A single character gains clarity and meaning by an orderly relationship of the space background which surrounds it. The greater the variety and distinction among respective background units, the clearer becomes the comprehension of a character as an individual expression or sign.[11]

Fables of Aesop, According to Sir Roger L'Estrange with drawings by Alexander Calder (Paris, 1931; New York, 1967), 1.

[11] Gyorgy Kepes, *The Language of Vision* (Chicago, 1948).

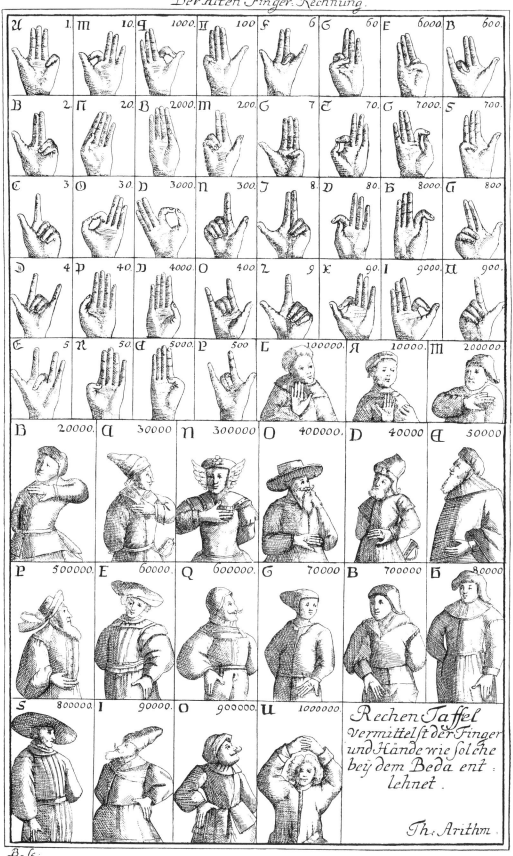

Jacob Leupold, *Theatrum Arithmetico-Geo-metricum*, (Leipzig, 1727), section 4, tab. I.

4 *Small Multiples*

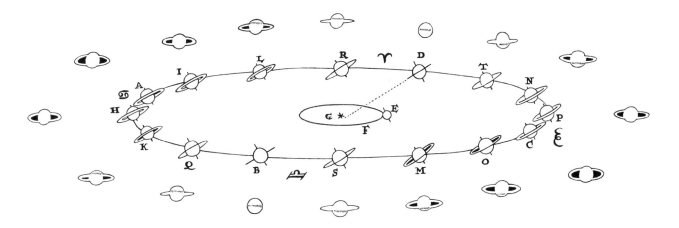

In this splendid 1659 drawing by Christiaan Huygens, the inner ellipse traces Earth's yearly journey around the Sun; the larger ellipse shows Saturn's orbit, viewed from the heavens. The outermost images depict Saturn as seen through telescopes located on Earth. All told, we have 32 Saturns, at different locations in three-space and from the perspective of two different observers—a superior *small multiple* design.

At the heart of quantitative reasoning is a single question: *Compared to what?* Small multiple designs, multivariate and data bountiful, answer directly by visually enforcing comparisons of changes, of the differences among objects, of the scope of alternatives. For a wide range of problems in data presentation, small multiples are the best design solution.

Illustrations of postage-stamp size are indexed by category or a label, sequenced over time like the frames of a movie, or ordered by a quantitative variable not used in the single image itself. Information slices are positioned within the eyespan, so that viewers make comparisons at a glance—uninterrupted visual reasoning. Constancy of design puts the emphasis on changes in data, not changes in data frames.

Christiaan Huygens, *Systema Saturnium* (The Hague, 1659), 55.

A. Ghizzo, B. Izrar, P. Betrand, E. Fijalkow, M. R. Feix, and M. Shoucri, "Stability of Bernstein-Greene-Kruskal Plasma Equilibria: Numerical Experiments Over a Long Time," *Physics of Fluids*, 31 (January 1988), 72-82. Viewing these illustrations upside down turns the mountains into valleys. Note also the two-space contour plots to the right of the three-space perspectives.

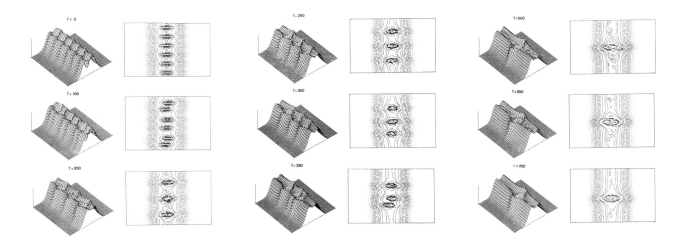

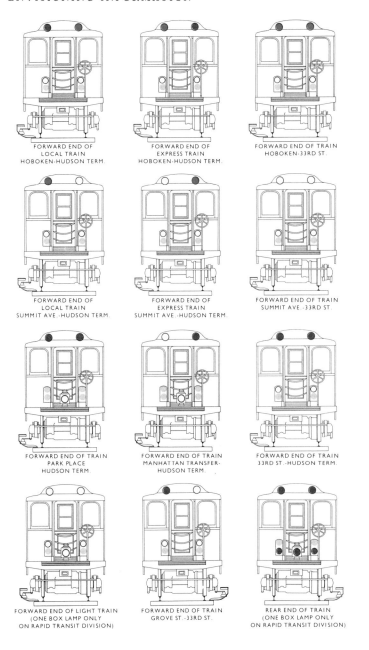

FORWARD END OF
LOCAL TRAIN
HOBOKEN-HUDSON TERM.

FORWARD END OF
EXPRESS TRAIN
HOBOKEN-HUDSON TERM.

FORWARD END OF TRAIN
HOBOKEN-33RD ST.

FORWARD END OF
LOCAL TRAIN
SUMMIT AVE.-HUDSON TERM.

FORWARD END OF
EXPRESS TRAIN
SUMMIT AVE.-HUDSON TERM.

FORWARD END OF TRAIN
SUMMIT AVE.-33RD ST.

FORWARD END OF TRAIN
PARK PLACE
HUDSON TERM.

FORWARD END OF TRAIN
MANHATTAN TRANSFER-
HUDSON TERM.

FORWARD END OF TRAIN
33RD ST.-HUDSON TERM.

FORWARD END OF LIGHT TRAIN
(ONE BOX LAMP ONLY
ON RAPID TRANSIT DIVISION)

FORWARD END OF TRAIN
GROVE ST.-33RD ST.

REAR END OF TRAIN
(ONE BOX LAMP ONLY
ON RAPID TRANSIT DIVISION)

Rules and Regulations for the Government of Employees of the Operating Department of the Hudson & Manhattan Railroad Company, Effective October 1st, 1923 (New York, 1923), 21. Redrawn.

SMALL multiples reveal, all at once, a scope of alternatives, a range of options. Above, varying signal lights on the ends of a train are entabled in a rulebook for railroad employees. Our redrawing mutes the repeated train outline and brings forward differentiating colors.

At far right, these photographs capture pressure, direction, and speed of the calligraphic brush as it draws a single Kana character. Images are indexed by time (→) and by dual camera angle (↑). The paired series of photographs link hand, brush, and character (top row). The second row shows pressure and bend of the brush-tip—and the consequent width of line. The sequence has a magical quality, reflecting a remark of Garry Winogrand, the photographer: "There is nothing as mysterious as a fact clearly described."

At right, Kayu Hirata, *Tsugi Shiki Shi*, volume 25 of *Shodo Giho Koza* [*Techniques in Calligraphy*] (Tokyo, 1974), 30. Above, without the aid of film, Mercator shows a similar sequence, the proper ordering of strokes in the formation of capital letters. Gerardus Mercator, *Literarum Latinarum, quas Italicas cursoriasque vocant, scribendarum ratio* [*The method of writing the Latin letters, which are called italic and cursive*] (Louvain, 1540), chapter 6.

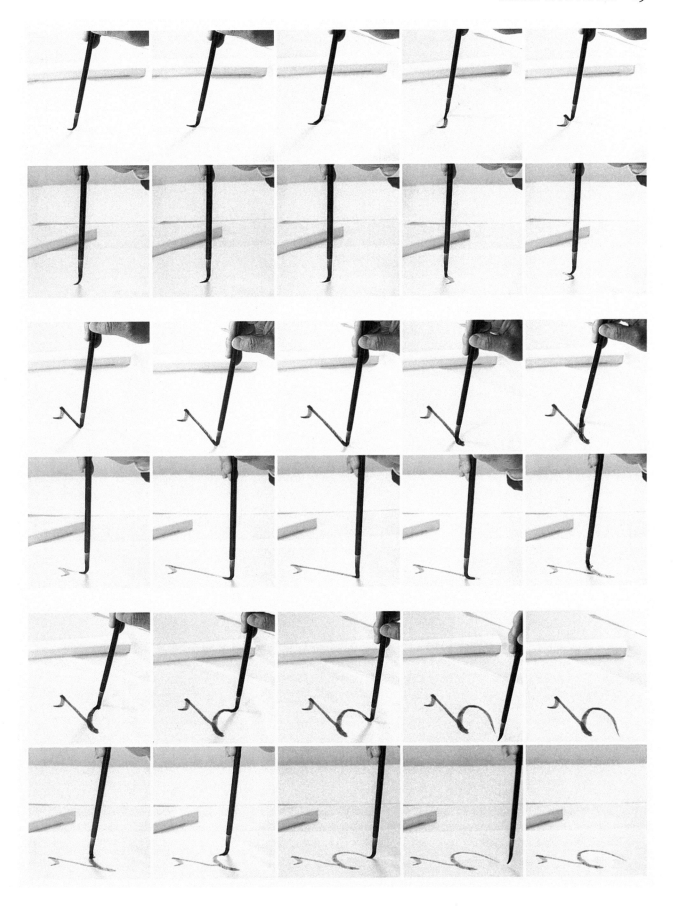

MURAL WITH BLUE BRUSHSTROKE

1. Detail of *The Dance* by Fernand Léger

2. Facade, Library of Celsus, Ephesus

To make *Mural with Blue Brushstroke*, Lichtenstein drew on sources ranging from the most exalted to the most banal. Classical architecture (2, 14) provided inspiration, as did the site itself (8, where painted windows align with real ones). Homages to twentieth-century masters abound: Léger's people (1), Kelly's color fields (6), Matisse's split philodendron form (9), Arp's silhouettes (10, echoed in a piece of Swiss cheese), De Kooning's brushstrokes (12), Stella's triangles and French curves (15), Johns's flagstones (16), and Braque's balusters (20). Art styles—like Abstract Expressionism (11, 12, and 13, the latter with its "perfect painting"), Cubism (20), and Art Deco (21)—and artist's tools (4, 5, and 15) appear. And bustling around amid all this high culture are images of everyday modern life, those perennial sources of fascination to Lichtenstein: sunbursts (3), copy books (17), advertisements (7), food and drink (10, 18), and, of course, comic strips (19).

7. Ad for Elgin watches, 1950s

8. Detail of the mural in place at Equitable

9. Henri Matisse, *Music*, 1939

13. Roy Lichtenstein, *Artist's Studio —Foot Medication*, 1974

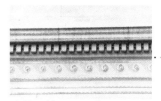

14. Entablature on downtown New York building

17. Classic black-and-white composition book

18. Roy Lichtenstein, *Still Life with Red Wine*, 1972

19. Roy Lichtenstein, *Knock Knock*, 1961

Roy Lichtenstein created "Mural with Blue Brushstroke" for the lobby of a building in New York. The large painting contains allusions to other works by Lichtenstein as well as many quotations (some a bit vaporous) from other artists. For a book describing the mural, Samuel

3. Roy Lichtenstein, *Placid Sea*, 1964

4. A gilded picture frame

5. The back of a painting, showing canvas, stretcher, and wedges

6. Ellsworth Kelly, *Red Blue Green*, 1963

10. Jean Arp, *Six White Forms and One Gray Form Make a Constellation on a Blue Ground*, 1953

11. Roy Lichtenstein, *Big Painting*, 1965

12. Willem de Kooning, *Greece on 8th Avenue*, 1958

15. Frank Stella, *Dove of Tanna*, 1977

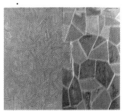

16. Jasper Johns, *End Paper*, 1976

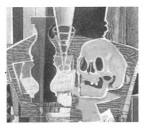

20. Georges Braque, *The Baluster*, 1938

21. Art Deco tray, designer and manufacturer unknown

Antupit (who was also responsible for the annotated invoice from the hospital) crafted this superb double-page spread, linking 21 small images from various sources to the mural at center. This design both isolates detail and places it in context.

Roy Lichtenstein: Mural with Blue Brushstroke, essay by Calvin Tomkins, photographs and interview by Bob Adelman (New York, 1988), 30-31.

Danforth, 1680

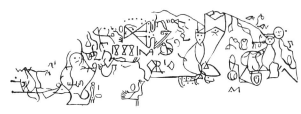

Baylies and Goodwin, 1790

Cotton Mather, 1712

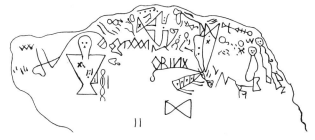

E. A. Kendall, 1807

Isaac Greenwood, 1730

Job Gardner, 1812

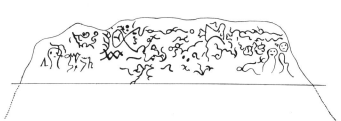

Stephen Sewell, 1768

Rhode Island Historical Society, 1830

James Winthrop, 1788

Henry R. Schoolcraft, 1854

WITH figures and pictographs chipped into stone, the Dighton Writing Rock sits near the Taunton River in southeastern Massachusetts. From 1680 onwards, observers sketched the inscriptions, with divergent results. Same rock, different views, arrayed here in a comparative small multiple. Some of these uncertain drawings, when sent off to European scholars, were then converted into far-reaching historical discoveries of startling visits to the New World. One researcher "triumphantly established" the marks as Scythian; a distinguished Orientalist detected the word *melek* (king) on the rock; others thought they saw Phoenician or Runic script. A Scandinavian antiquary translated the drawings into an account of a pre-Columbian sojourn to America by a party of Thorfinn the Hopeful. Since the writing resembles that on the Indian God Rock hundreds of miles southwest, such logic places the Vikings far inland, deep into what is now West Virginia and Ohio. All this scholarship of wishful thinking denies priority to the original Native-American residents; local experts conclude that the marks are Algonquin.[1]

A focused small multiple, below, shows the history of variations in the ghost-like figure, enforcing comparisons over time (the ghosts even could be spaced in proportion to the date they were drawn):

[1] Charles Christian Rafn, *Antiquités Américaines d'après les Monuments Historiques des Islandais et des Anciens Scandinaves* (Copenhagen, 1845); Henry R. Schoolcraft, *Information Respecting the History, Condition, and Prospects of the Indian Tribes of the United States*, Part IV (Philadelphia, 1854), plate 14. Garrick Mallery, "Picture-Writing of the American Indians," in *Tenth Annual Report of the Bureau of Ethnology to the Secretary of the Smithsonian Institution, 1888-89* (Washington, DC, 1893), 762-764, and plate LIV; redrawn. John Michell, *Megalithomania* (Ithaca, New York, 1982), 145, on local expert opinion. Other instances of divergent interpretations of ambiguous visual signals include variable readings of the floor plan of San Carlo alle Quattro Fontane in Rome; see Rudolf Arnheim, *New Essays on the Psychology of Art* (Berkeley, 1986), 301-309; and Leo Steinberg, *Borromini's San Carlo alle Quattro Fontane* (New York, 1977). The melancholy history of the canals of Mars seen by Schiaparelli and Lowell is documented in William Sheehan, *Planets and Perception: Telescopic Views and Interpretations, 1609-1909* (Tuscon, Arizona, 1988).

DURING the last 1,260 years in China, where did poets flourish? How many poets? And have their birthplaces changed over the years? Four maps, based on an inherently imperfect historical record, address these prominent questions.

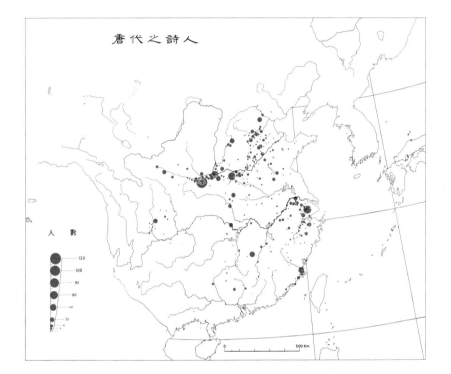

Redrawn from Chen Cheng-Siang, *An Historical and Cultural Atlas of China* (Tokyo, 1981), maps 36, 50, 62, and 82.

Birthplaces of the 2,625 Tang poets, 618-907

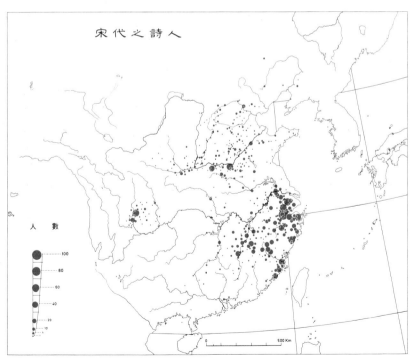

Birthplaces of the 2,377 Sung poets, 969-1279

Shown is the geographic distribution of poets (grand total 10,086) during four dynasties, with their birthplaces shifting through centuries toward southeast China and concentrating—as is the case for so much human activity—in a relatively few areas.

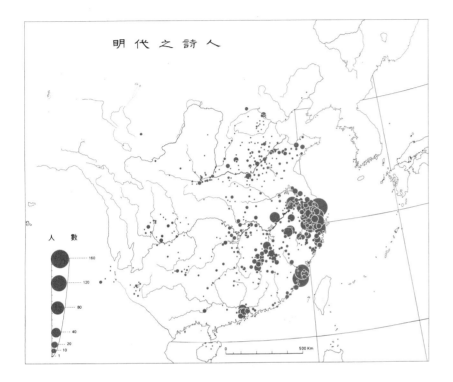

Birthplaces of the 3,005 Ming poets, 1368-1644

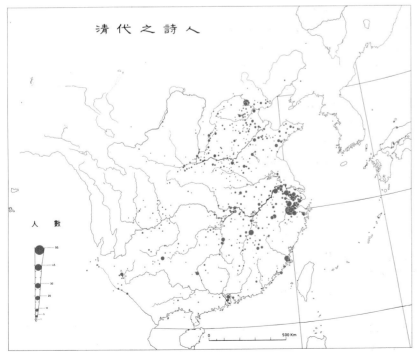

Birthplaces of the 2,079 Ching poets, 1644-1911

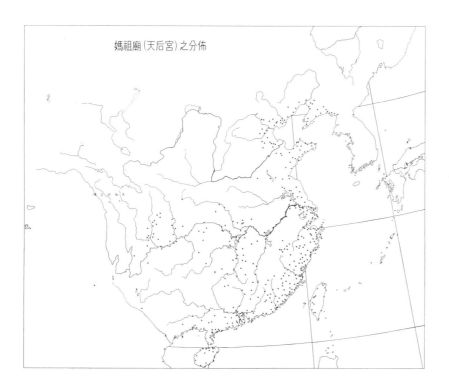

媽祖廟 (天后宮) 之分佈

Redrawn from Chen Cheng-Siang, *An Historical and Cultural Atlas of China* (Tokyo, 1981), map 91.

[2] A recent account is by James L. Watson, "Standardizing the Gods: The Promotion of T'ien Hou ('Empress of Heaven') Along the South China Coast, 960-1960," in David Johnson, Andrew J. Nathan, and Evelyn S. Rawski, eds., *Popular Culture in Late Imperial China* (Berkeley, 1985), 292-324.

Ta-ch'eng Ch'eng, *Ma-tsu chuan* (Taipei, 1955), illustration 29.

And, finally, a map of distribution of temples of Matsu (T'ien Hou), the most famous sea goddess of China. With a sterling reputation for miracles, she receives prayers of fishermen and sailors during stormy weather; and when the sea is as dark as ink, she provides a torch on the top of the mast to guide small boats to safety. In recent times, the story goes, one mother (an alleged descendant of the goddess) left her child at a temple while going to work on the farm, saying "Sea Goddess, please take heed." Matsu's reaction to supervising a day-care facility was not recorded. Our display here, growing from surpassingly incomplete data, marks prefectures with a temple honoring Matsu.[2] But we are unable to make the long-awaited comparisons among geographic distributions of sea-goddess temples and birthplaces of Tang, Sung, Ming, and Ching poets—because the poets are stranded over on the two preceding pages. *Comparisons must be enforced within the scope of the eyespan*, a fundamental point occasionally forgotten in practice.

The struggle between maintenance of context and enforcement of comparison is reflected in a 19th-century topographic diagram at right. Surveying lengths of the world's rivers, the chart hangs them out, in parallel more or less, while still retaining specifics of place-names, lakes, and river branches. Note the various sequences of lakes, here linearly arranged. Without such detail, this is just another decorated bar chart. Some ardent typography sets oceans rippling at top. The juxtaposed mountains are less successful, too arbitrary in their relocation, and too stylized and lacking the nice local particulars of the rivers.

Joseph Hutchins Colton, *Johnson's New Illustrated Family Atlas with Physical Geography* (New York, 1864), 10-11.

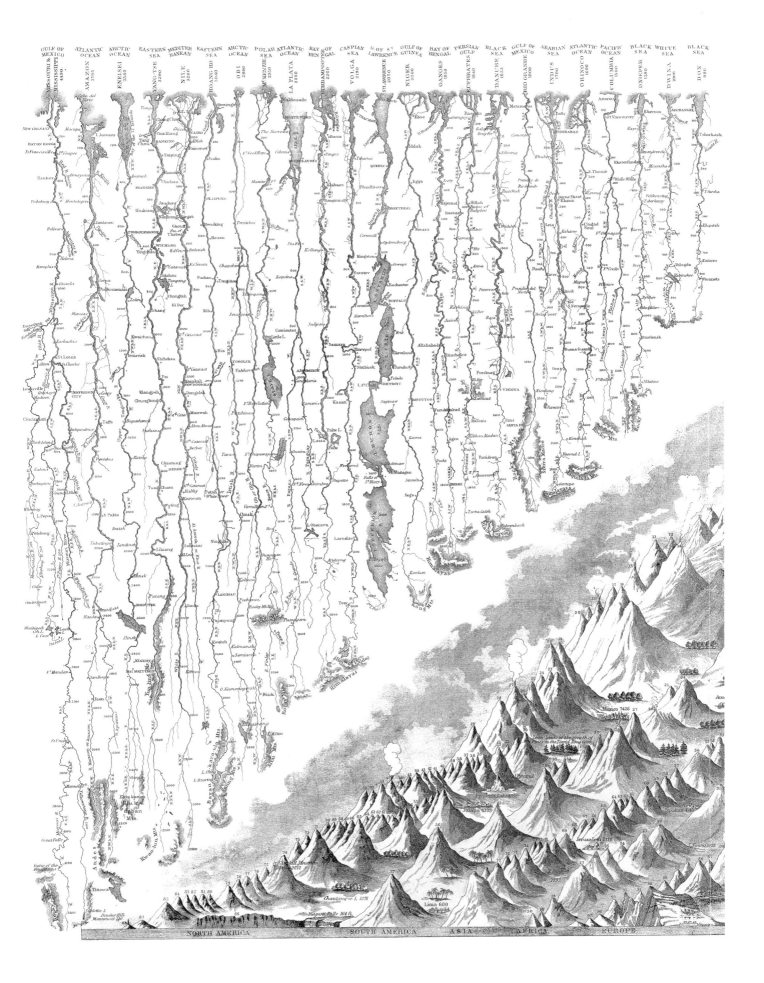

Simultaneous two-dimensional indexing of the multiplied image, flatland within flatland, significantly deepens displays, with little added complication in reading. These neurometric maps record distributions of brain electrical activity, arraying data over a matrix of color images— with frequency bands (delta, theta, alpha, and beta) sorting the columns, and individual diagnosis forming the rows. The contour lines depict only the average differences (normalized z-scores) of the row *group* compared to a healthy reference *group*, and thus do not show overlaps or extreme outlying values of all the *individual* members of each group.[3] Graphically, this recursive design resembles the Los Angeles smog chart that we saw in Chapter 1, where maps were themselves spread on two dimensions, type of pollution and time of day.

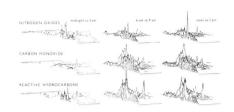

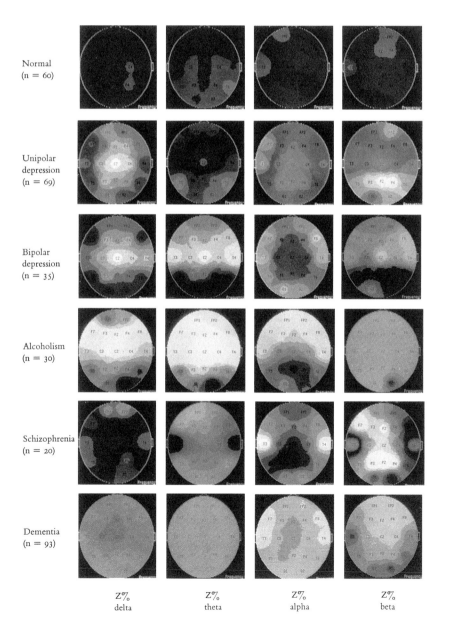

[3] E. R. John, L. S. Prichep, J. Fridman, and P. Easton, "Neurometrics: Computer-Assisted Differential Diagnosis of Brain Dysfunctions," *Science*, 239 (January 8, 1988), 162-169. The authors conclude: "Healthy persons display only chance deviations beyond the predicted ranges. . . . Patients with neurological impairments, subtle cognitive dysfunctions, or psychiatric disorders show a high incidence of abnormal values. The magnitude of the deviations increases with clinical severity. Different disorders are characterized by distinctive profiles of abnormal brain electrical features. . . . These methods may provide independent criteria for diagnostic validity, evaluations of treatment efficacy, and more individualized therapy."

John Jackson, *The Practical Fly-Fisher; More Particularly for Grayling or Umber* (London, 1854), plate VIII, at 26–27, insects and flies for July and August.

In our neurometric example at left, the dark colors surrounding each image generate disruptive white stripes. Locations can be signaled by nearly silent methods, as above, where an implicit grid pairs each insect with its fly-fishing simulation. And the limited but focused color here is more effective than strong rainbow colors, for reasons now to be revealed.

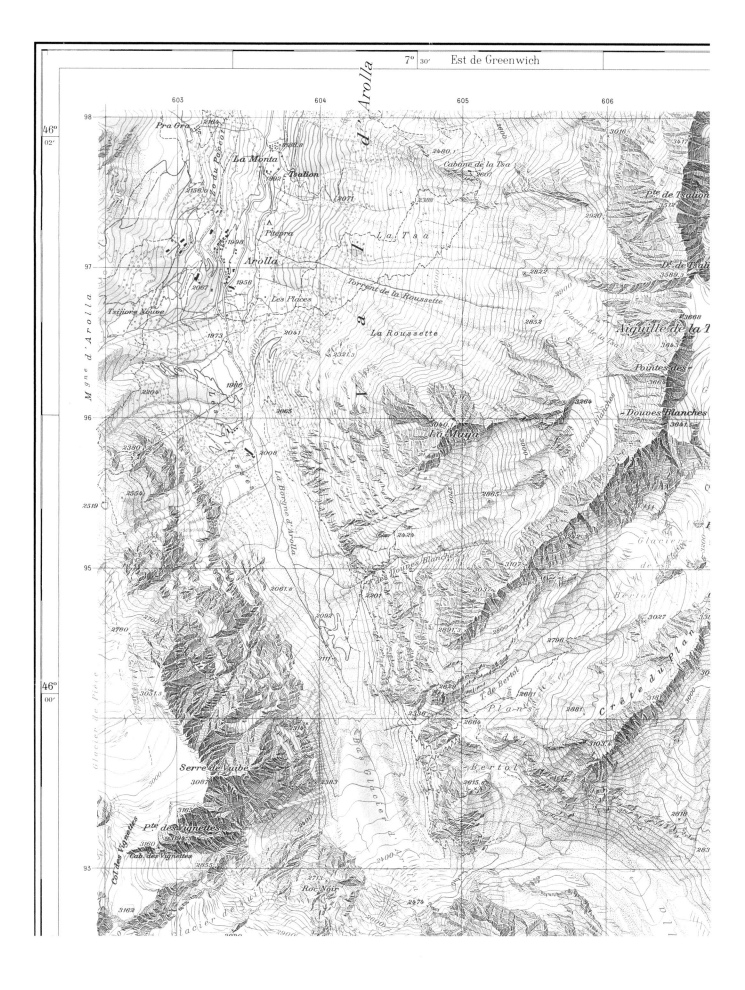

5   Color and Information

In representing and communicating information, how are we to benefit from color's great dominion? Human eyes are exquisitely sensitive to color variations: a trained colorist can distinguish among 1,000,000 colors, at least when tested under contrived conditions of pairwise comparison. Some 20,000 colors are accessible to many viewers, with the constraints for practical applications set by the early limits of human visual memory rather than the capacity to discriminate locally among adjacent tints. For encoding abstract information, however, more than 20 or 30 colors frequently produce not diminishing but negative returns.

Tying color to information is as elementary and straightforward as color technique in art, "To paint well is simply this: to put the right color in the right place," in Paul Klee's ironic prescription.[1] The often scant benefits derived from coloring data indicate that even putting a good color in a good place is a complex matter. Indeed, so difficult and subtle that avoiding catastrophe becomes the first principle in bringing color to information: *Above all, do no harm.*

[1] Paul Klee, *Notebooks: The Thinking Eye*, translated by Ralph Manheim (London, 1961; Basel, 1956), volume 1, 39, n. 1.

At work in this fine Swiss mountain map are the fundamental uses of color in information design: *to label* (color as noun), *to measure* (color as quantity), *to represent or imitate reality* (color as representation), and *to enliven or decorate* (color as beauty). Here color *labels* by distinguishing water from stone and glacier from field, *measures* by indicating altitude with contour and rate of change by darkening, *imitates reality* with river blues and shadow hachures, and visually *enlivens* the topography quite beyond what could be done in black and white alone.

Note the many finely crafted details: changes in the color of contour lines as the background shifts, interplay of light and shadow in areas of glacial activity, and color typography. The black-ink-only area at the bottom, though not an optimized monochrome design, gives a sense of the overwhelming informational benefits of color, when it is at its best.

Matterhorn, Landeskarte der Schweiz, 1347, Bundesamt für Landestopographie (Wabern, 1983), scale 1:25,000.

The Swiss maps are excellent because they are *governed by good ideas and executed with superb craft*. Ideas not only guide work, but also help defend our designs (by providing *reasons* for choices) against arbitrary taste preferences. Strategies for how color can serve information are set out in Eduard Imhof's classic *Cartographic Relief Presentation*, which describes the design practices for the Swiss maps. The first two principles seek to minimize color damage:

> *First rule:* Pure, bright or very strong colors have loud, unbearable effects when they stand unrelieved over large areas adjacent to each other, but extraordinary effects can be achieved when they are used sparingly on or between dull background tones. "Noise is not music. Only a piano allows a crescendo and then a forte, and only on a quiet background can a colorful theme be constructed." The organization of the earth's surface facilitates graphic solutions of this type in maps. Extremes of any type—such as highest land zones and deepest sea troughs, temperature maxima and minima—generally enclose small areas only. If one limits strong, heavy, rich, and solid colors to the small areas of extremes, then expressive and beautiful patterns occur. If one gives all, especially large areas, glaring, rich colors, the pictures have brilliant, disordered, confusing and unpleasant effects.

> *Second rule:* The placing of light, bright colors mixed with white next to each other usually produces unpleasant results, especially if the colors are used for large areas.[2]

Violation of this counsel yields the exuberantly bad example below. All this strong color, especially the surrounding blue, generates a strange puffy white band, making it the map's dominant visual statement, with some alarming shapes at lower left. These colors are dark in value, and inevitably we have significant $1 + 1 = 3$ effects again, at visual war with the heavily encoded information.

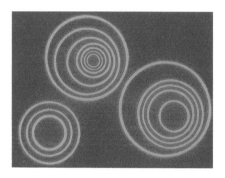

[2] Note the after-images and vibration resulting from these strong colors (complementary, equal in value), an example from Josef Albers, *The Interaction of Color* (New Haven, 1963), "Vibrating Boundaries," folder XXII-1. The quotation is part of a longer list of color principles in Eduard Imhof, *Cartographic Relief Presentation* (Berlin, 1982), edited and translated by H. J. Steward from Imhof's *Kartographische Geländedarstellung* (Berlin, 1965), 72. The internal quotation is from H. Windisch, *Schule der Farbenphotographie* (Seebruck, 6th edition, 1958). The color logic is similar to that for emphasis in music: "Without accent there is no life. The beat becomes monotonous and wearisome. Music without accent lacks coherence, and movement becomes aimless where there is no impulse. Conversely, if every note, word or movement is stressed, the result has even less meaning." Ann Driver, *Music and Movement* (London, 1936), 34.

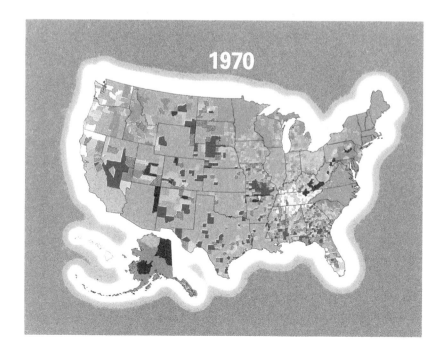

"Primary Home Heating Fuel, by Counties of the United States: 1950, 1960, 1970," GE-70, Bureau of the Census, United States Department of Commerce (Washington, DC, n.d.). This series of maps also includes first-rate efforts, including the well-known "flashlight map" of population density.

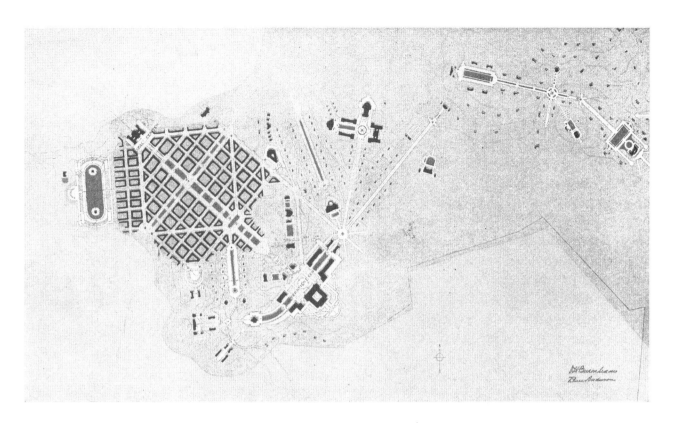

Along with its critique of color-clutter, Imhof's first rule contains an important constructive idea: *color spots against a light gray or muted field highlight and italicize data, and also help to weave an overall harmony.* Daniel Burnham's architectural drawing shows the vitality of small color spots on large muted backgrounds: coherent, vivid and textured but without clutter, the right color in the right place. The 1909 *Plan of Chicago* contains several other drawings the equal of that shown here—with skillful color illuminating architectural drawings and maps.

Applying a single mark, a strong but transparent spot, Jan Tschichold labels his rejection of the classical central axis typography and design, in favor of the asymmetric layout at right.

Daniel H. Burnham, "Plan for a Summer Capital of the Philippine Islands, at Baguio," in Daniel H. Burnham and Edward H. Bennett, edited by Charles Moore, *Plan of Chicago* (Chicago, 1909), 28.

Jan Tschichold, *Die Neue Typographie* (Berlin, 1928), 214-215. Redrawn.

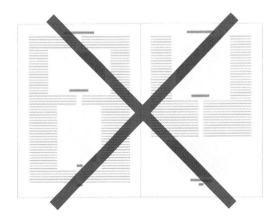

COLOR serves as a label most nobly of all in Oliver Byrne's 1847 edition of Euclid's *Geometry*. This truly visual Euclid discards the letter-coding native to geometry texts. In a proof, each element names itself by consistent shape, color, and orientation; instead of talking about angle DEF, the angle is *shown*—appropriately enough for geometry. Below, we see an orthodox march through the Pythagorean theorem; too much time must be spent puzzling over an alphabetic macaroni of 63 encoded links between diagram and proof. At far right, the visual Pythagoras. Ruari McLean described Byrne's book as "one of the oddest and most beautiful books of the whole [19th] century . . . a decided complication of Euclid, but a triumph for Charles Whittingham [the printer]."[3] A close look, however, indicates that Byrne's design clarifies the overly indirect and complicated Euclid, at least for certain readers.[4]

[3] Ruari McLean, *Victorian Book Design and Colour Printing* (New York, 1963), 51. See also Ruari McLean, *A Book is Not a Book* (Denver: University of Denver Graduate School of Librarianship, 1974).

[4] The classical Chinese mathematics book, the *Chou Pei Suan Ching* (ca -600 to +300), used but a single diagram for proof of the "Pythagorean" theorem. According to Needham, "in the time of Liu and Chao [ca +200], it was coloured, the small central square being yellow and the surrounding rectangles red." [Joseph Needham with Wang Ling, *Science and Civilisation in China: Mathematics and the Sciences of the Heavens and the Earth* (Cambridge, 1959), volume 3, 22-23, 95-97.] The logic is

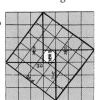

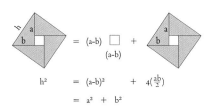

$$h^2 = (a-b)^2 + 4\left(\tfrac{ab}{2}\right)$$
$$= a^2 + b^2$$

immediate, unlike the notoriously circuitous Euclid (Schopenhauer, *Sämmtliche Werke*, I. §15, described Euclid's Pythagoras as "a proof walking on stilts, nay, a mean, underhand proof"). And, pleasingly, Heath declares that the Chinese proof has "no specifically Greek colouring." [Thomas L. Heath, *Euclid: The Thirteen Books of the Elements* (Cambridge, 1926), volume I, 355.] See also the very special collection of 367 proofs, Elisha S. Loomis, *The Pythagorean Proposition* (Ann Arbor, 1940).

THEOREM 27. (Pythagoras' Theorem.)

In any right-angled triangle, the square on the hypotenuse is equal to the sum of the squares on the sides **containing** the right angle.

Given ∠BAC is a right angle.

To prove the square on BC = the square on BA + the square on AC.

Let ABHK, ACMN, BCPQ be the squares on AB, AC, BC.

Join CH, AQ. Through A, draw AXY parallel to BQ, cutting BC, QP at X, Y.

Since ∠BAC and ∠BAK are right angles, KA and AC are in the same straight line.

Again ∠HBA = 90° = ∠QBC.

Add to each ∠ABC, ∴ ∠HBC = ∠ABQ.

In the △s HBC, ABQ.

HB = AB, sides of square.

CB = QB, sides of square.

∠HBC = ∠ABQ, proved.

∴ △HBC = △ABQ (2 sides, inc. angle).

Now △HBC and square HA are on the same base HB and between the same parallels HB, KAC ;

∴ △HBC = ½ square HA.

Also △ABQ and rectangle BQYX are on the same base BQ and between the same parallels BQ, AXY.

∴ △ABQ = ½ rect. BQYX.

∴ square HA = rect. BQYX.

Similarly, by joining AP, BM, it can be shown that square MA = rect. CPYX ;

∴ square HA + square MA = rect. BQYX + rect. CPYX

= square BP.   Q.E.D.

FIG. 163.

C.V. Durell, *Elementary Geometry* (London, 1936), 119. For redesign of Durell's page in Gill Sans, see Peggy Lang, "Interpretative Typography Applied to School Geometry," *Typography*, 3 (Summer 1937); and Grant Shipcott, *Typographical Periodicals Between the Wars: A Critique of The Fleuron, Signature and Typography* (Oxford, 1980), 65.

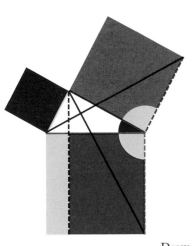

N   a   right   angled   triangle the ſquare

on the hypotenuſe ——— is equal to

the ſum of the ſquares of the ſides, (———

and ———) .

On ——— , ——— and ——— deſcribe ſquares,

Draw --------- || --------- alſo draw ——— and ——— .

 = , To each add ∴  ,

——— = --------- and ——— = --------- ;

 = .

Again, becauſe ——— || ---------

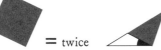 = twice , and 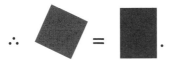 = twice ;

∴ = .

In the ſame manner it may be ſhown

that = ;

hence 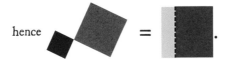 = .

Redrawn from Oliver Byrne, *The First Six Books of the Elements of Euclid in which coloured diagrams and symbols are used instead of letters for the greater ease of learners* (London, 1847), 48-49.

Below, instructions for circumscribing a square on a circle, with a typically roundabout Euclidean proof verifying that ☐ really is square. Byrne's colors keep in mind the knowledge to be communicated, color *for* information. Use of the primary colors and black provides maximum differentiation (no four colors differ more). The yellow, broken with orange, is darkened in value, sharpening the definition of its edge against white paper; and the blue is relatively light (on a value scale of blues), reinforcing its distance from black. In the diagrams, the least-used color is black, and it is carefully avoided for large, solid elements—adding to the overall coherence of the proofs by muting unnecessary contrasts. Spacious leading of type assists integration of text and figure, and also unifies the page by creating *lines* of type (instead of the solid masses usually formed by bodies of straight text) similar in visual presence to the geometric lines and shapes.

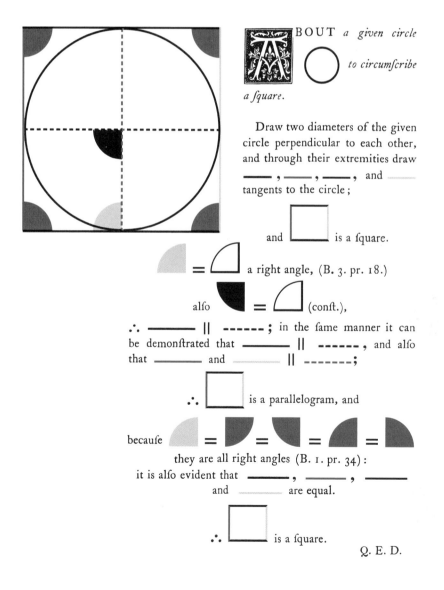

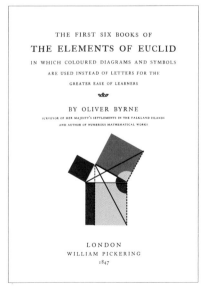

THE FIRST SIX BOOKS OF
THE ELEMENTS OF EUCLID
IN WHICH COLOURED DIAGRAMS AND SYMBOLS
ARE USED INSTEAD OF LETTERS FOR THE
GREATER EASE OF LEARNERS

BY OLIVER BYRNE
SURVEYOR OF HER MAJESTY'S SETTLEMENTS IN THE FALKLAND ISLANDS
AND AUTHOR OF NUMEROUS MATHEMATICAL WORKS

LONDON
WILLIAM PICKERING
1847

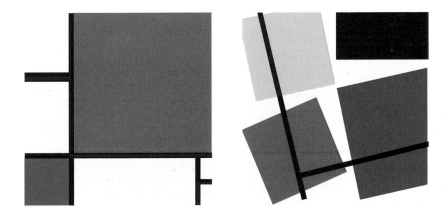

Piet Mondrian, *Composition with Red, Yellow and Blue*, 1930.

Theo van Doesburg, *Simultaneous Counter-Composition*, 1929-1930.

Design of these 292 pages of Euclid—drawn in 1847 by Her Majesty's surveyor of the Falkland Islands and also school mathematics teacher, Oliver Byrne—anticipates the pure primary colors, asymmetrical layout, angularity, lightness of plentiful empty space, and non-representational (abstract, "denaturalized") shapes characteristic of 20th-century Neo-Plasticism and De Stijl painting.[5] *And it is Euclid, too.* Only the decorative initial capital letters (wood-engraved by Mary Byfield) appear now as pre-modern . . . or, for that matter, post-modern.

This redrawing below of part of Pythagoras couples Byrne's visual method with conventional letter-encoding. Deflecting the fussiness that often results from redundant signals, the intermingling here of two labeling techniques seems to speed recognition of geometric elements as the eye moves between diagram and proof. Such a combination allows viewers to choose how they link up the text with the diagram, and it is likely that both methods will be used together.

[5] Piet Mondrian presented principles of Neo-Plasticism in 1926: "(1) The plastic medium should be the flat plane or the rectangular prism in primary colors (red, blue, and yellow) and in non-color (white, black, and gray). . . . (2) There must be an equivalence of plastic means. Different in size and color, they should nevertheless have equal value. In general, equilibrium involves a large uncolored surface or an empty space, and a rather small colored surface . . . . (4) Abiding equilibrium is achieved through opposition and is expressed by the straight line (limit of the plastic means) in its principal opposition, i.e., the right angle. . . . (6) All symmetry shall be excluded." One version of the essay, "Home—Street—City," is found in Michel Seuphor, *Piet Mondrian: Life and Work* (New York, 1956), 166-168; see also *The New Art—The New Life: The Collected Writings of Piet Mondrian*, edited and translated by Harry Holtzman and Martin S. James (Boston, 1986), 205-212.

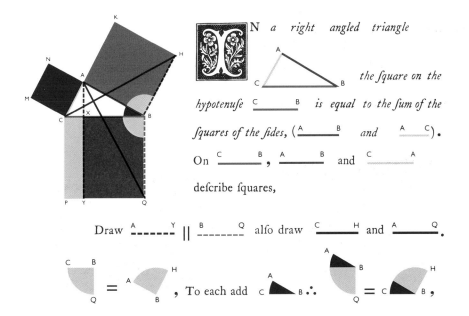

IN all 50 or so systems of color organization, every color is located in three space: described by *hue, saturation, and value* in Munsell and other spatial-perceptual classifications; by *red, green, and blue* components in various additive methods for video displays; and by *cyan, magenta, and yellow* components in subtractive methods for printing inks. A variety of color systems, but always three dimensions.

Can color's inherently multidimensional quality be used to express multidimensional information? And can viewers understand, or learn to understand, such displays? A good place to start on a video display terminal is to spread data-points over flatland for two dimensions and then light up each point by red, green, and blue (RGB) components,

Colin Ware and John C. Beatty, "Using Color as a Tool in Discrete Data Analysis," Computer Science Department, University of Waterloo, report CS-85-21 (August 1985); and "Using Color Dimensions to Display Data Dimensions," *Human Factors*, 30 (1988), 127–142. Success is reported for locating simple clusters of data. For serious data analysis the method depends on how well viewers can visualize a particular color as a three-dimensional location.

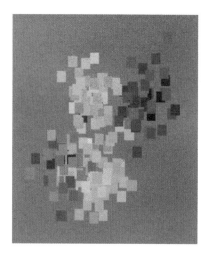 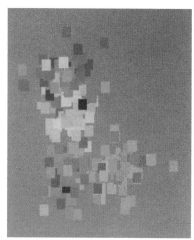 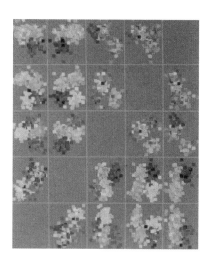

in proportion to values taken by three additional variables. At right, a five by five scatterplot matrix shows all X-Y pairs. Note color clusters of data, assemblies of three-dimensional similarity (on RGB variables) spread on the X-Y plane, an obvious improvement over black-only dots.

Color's multidimensionality can also enliven and inform what users must face at computer terminals, although some color applied to display screens has made what should be a straight-forward tool into something that looks like a grim parody of a video game:

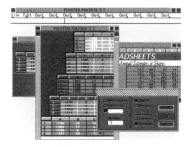  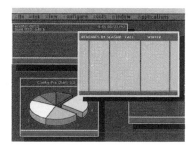

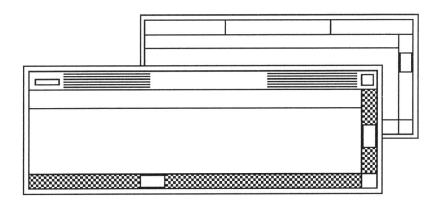

Shown above are conventional graphical interfaces, with scroll bars, multiple windows, and computer administrative debris. Closely-spaced, dark grid lines generate 1 + 1 = 3 clutter, with noise growing from the overscan borders (the surrounding dead area of a video tube). Noise is costly, since computer displays are low-resolution devices, working at extremely thin data densities, 1/10 to 1/1000 of a map or book page. This reflects the essential dilemma of a computer display: at every screen are two powerful information-processing capabilities, human and computer. Yet all communication between the two must pass through the low-resolution, narrow-band video display terminal, which chokes off fast, precise, and complex communication.

Color can improve the information resolution of a computer screen.[6] First, by softening the bright-white background, color calms video glare, the effect of staring at a light bulb. Below, color defines edges and allows a simple and elegant *de-gridded* design. For framing fields, the appropriate color should be *light in value* (muting 1 + 1 = 3 effects), and, at the same time, relatively *intense and saturated* (to give a strong visual signal for an active window). Yellow is the only color that satisfies this joint requirement. Thus a two-dimensional display task is handled by two visual dimensions of a single color:

[6] See James D. Foley, Victor L. Wallace, and Peggy Chan, "The Human Factors of Computer Graphics Interaction Techniques," *Computer Graphics and Applications* (November 1984), 13-48; Ben Shneiderman, *Designing the User Interface* (Reading, Massachusetts, 1987); Philip K. Robertson, "Visualizing Color Gamuts: A User Interface for the Effective Use of Perceptual Color Spaces in Data Displays," *Computer Graphics and Applications* (September 1988), 50-64; and also Edward R. Tufte, *Visual Design of the User Interface* (Armonk, New York, 1989). In contrast to the low-resolution and garish color of the computer screen, consider the stamp, with a sometimes delicate use of color (by varying densities of engraving) and fine detail:

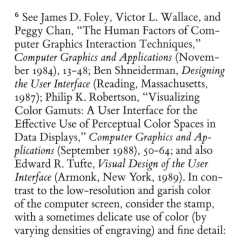

WHAT palette of colors should we choose to represent and illuminate information? A grand strategy is to *use colors found in nature*, especially those on the lighter side, such as blues, yellows, and grays of sky and shadow. Nature's colors are familiar and coherent, possessing a widely accepted harmony to the human eye—and their source has a certain definitive authority. A palette of nature's colors helps suppress produc-

Gretchen Garner, *A Grove of Birches*, photographs, 1988.

tion of garish and content-empty colorjunk. Local emphasis for data is then given by means of spot highlights of strong color woven through the serene background. Eduard Imhof develops this theme, with his characteristic mix of cartographic science and art:

> *Third rule*: Large area background or base-colors should do their work most quietly, allowing the smaller, bright areas to stand out most vividly, if the former are muted, grayish or neutral. For this very good reason, *gray* is regarded in painting to be one of the prettiest, most important and most versatile of colors. Strongly muted colors, mixed with gray, provide the best background for the colored theme. This philosophy applies equally to map design.

> *Fourth rule*: If a picture is composed of two or more large, enclosed areas in different colors, then the picture falls apart. Unity will be maintained, however, if the colors of one area are repeatedly intermingled in the other, if the colors are interwoven carpet-fashion throughout the other. All colors of the main theme should be scattered like islands in the background color. The complex nature of the earth's surface leads to enclosed colored areas, all over maps. They are the islands in the sea, the lakes on continents, they are lowlands, highlands, etc., which often also appear in thematic maps, and provide a desirable amount of disaggregation, interpretation and reiteration within the image.[7]

[7] Eduard Imhof, *Cartographic Relief Presentation* (Berlin, 1982), edited and translated by H. J. Steward from Imhof's *Kartographische Geländedarstellung* (Berlin, 1965), 72. Here what should be strictly cartographic and information design arguments are pushed too far toward a general theory of aesthetics. Mondrian, Malevich, and many others routinely violate the fourth rule; the problem is with the rule not Mondrian.

Of course color brings to information more than just codes naming visual nouns—color is a natural quantifier, with a perceptually continuous (in value and saturation) span of incredible fineness of distinction, at a precision comparable to most measurement. For data then as for art: "And what tremendous possibilities for the variation of meaning are offered by the combination of colors. . . . What variations from the smallest shading to the glowing symphony of color. What perspectives in the dimension of meaning!" wrote Paul Klee.[8] In practice everything is not this wonderful, given the frequently uneasy translations from number to corresponding color and thence to human readings and interpretations.

The General Bathymetric Chart of the Oceans records ocean depth (bathymetric tints) and land height (hypsometric tints) in 21 steps— with "the deeper or higher, the darker" serving as the visual metaphor for coloring. Shown are the great ocean trenches of the western Pacific and Japan Sea. Numbered contours outline color fields, improving accuracy of reading. Nearly transparent gray tracks, on a visual plane apart from the bathymetric tints, trace paths of sounding lines (outside those areas of extremely detailed surveys, such as ports and along coast lines). Every color mark on this map signals four variables: latitude, longitude, sea or land, and depth or altitude measured in meters.

[8] Paul Klee, *On Modern Art* (London, 1948), translated by Paul Findlay from *Über die moderne Kunst* (Bern, 1945), 39-41.

General Bathymetric Chart of the Oceans, International Hydrographic Organization (Ottawa, Canada, 5th edition, 1984), 5.06.

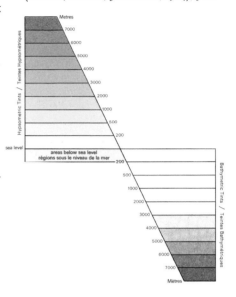

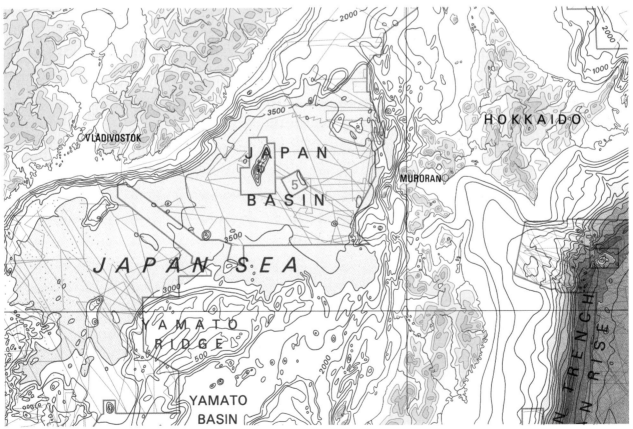

In the ocean map, quantities are shown by a *value* scale, progressing from light to dark blue. Although easy to learn and remember, value scales may be vulnerable to the inaccuracies of reading provoked by disturbing contextual effects, shown above, of edge fluting and simultaneous contrast. A widely-used alternative is a scale of rainbow colors, replacing the clear visual sequence of light to dark with the disorderly red, orange, yellow, green, blue, indigo, and violet—an encoding that now and then reduces perplexed viewers to mumbling color names and the numbers they represent, perversely contrary to Paul Valéry's axiom, "To see is to forget the name of the thing one sees." Despite our experiences with the spectrum in science textbooks and rainbows, the mind's eye does not readily give an order to ROYGBIV.[9] In the face of this rainbow encipherment, viewers must turn to other cues (contour, edge, labels) in order to see and interpret data.

[9] Controlled variations in hue, however, help extend value scales, increasing fineness of differentiation and yet still giving viewers a sense of natural visual sequence.

ANY color coding of quantity (whether based on variations in hue, value, or saturation) is potentially sensitive to interactive contextual effects. These perceived color shifts, while an infrequent threat to accuracy of reading in day-to-day information design, are surprising and vivid—suggesting that color differences should not be relied upon as the sole method for sending a message amidst a mosaic of complex and variable data. Here the same color (in the central squares) looks quite different when placed in slightly different circumstances. The small squares are shifted so as to match the opposite surround—a fine

visual touch. Perhaps even more stunning are arrangements of color fields that make two different colors look alike. Albers describes this as a *subtraction* of color: "Repeated . . . experiments with adjacent colors will show that any ground subtracts its own hue from colors which it carries and therefore influences."[10] How different the colors of the small squares above look against a uniform white field:

Can these interactions of color *benefit* information displays? Not often, but, in this conventional road map, the perceived visual palette used for labels is extended, without the expense of printing an additional flat color. The thin red line (smaller roads) changes to a deeper red when flanked by parallel blue stripes in the code for larger roads.

Color itself is subtle and exacting. And, furthermore, the process of translating perceived color marks on paper into quantitative data residing in the viewer's mind is beset by uncertainties and complexities.[11] These translations are nonlinear (thus gamma curves), often noisy and idiosyncratic, with plenty of differences in perception found among viewers (including several percent who are color-deficient).[12,13]

MULTIPLE signals will help escape from the swamp of perceptual shifts and other ambiguities in reading. Redundant and partially overlapping methods of data representation can yield a sturdy design, responding in one way or another to potential visual complications—with, however, a resulting danger of fussy, cluttered, insecure, committee-style design. A crystalline, lucid redundancy will do.

[10] Josef Albers, *Interaction of Color* (New Haven, 1963), 28. In reading these color comparisons, Albers suggests "For a proper comparison, we must see them simultaneously, not alternatingly. The latter way, a repeated looking forth and back, produces changing and disturbing after-images which make a comparison under equal conditions impossible. For a simultaneous comparison, therefore, we must focus at a *center* between the 2 rectangles, and for a sufficient length of time." (*Interaction of Color: Commentary*, 16, italics added.) Students of printing may wish to note that reproduction of the various examples here required 23 separate flat colors for this signature.

[11] See Günter Wyszecki and W. S. Stiles, *Color Science: Concepts and Methods, Quantitative Data and Formulae* (New York, 2nd edition, 1982); and, a book better than its title, Deane B. Judd and Günter Wyszecki, *Color in Business, Science and Industry* (New York, 3rd edition, 1975).

[12] Because of color-deficient vision, it is best to avoid making crucial data distinctions depend on the difference between red and green. See Leo M. Hurvich, *Color Vision* (Sunderland, Massachusetts, 1981).

[13] Also, the specific details of linking color to number must be decided in relation to the information itself, taking into account the frequency distribution of the data, what aspects of the data are to come forward, and the delineation of important cutpoints. For a good analysis of these issues, see Eduard Imhof, *Cartographic Relief Presentation* (Berlin, 1982), translated by H. J. Steward from Imhof's *Kartographische Geländedarstellung* (Berlin, 1965), 312-324.

Transparent and effective deployment of redundant signals requires, first, the *need*—an ambiguity or confusion in seeing a data display that can in fact be diminished by multiplicity—and, second, the *appropriate choice of design technique* (from among all the various methods of signal reinforcement) that will work to minimize the ambiguity of reading.[14] Disregard of these conspicuous distinctions will propagate a gratuitous multiplicity. Several examples, illustrating mutual interplay of color and contour, give our verbal pronouncements a visual reality.

The ocean map exemplifies a sensitive multiplicity: the color fields which encode depth are in turn delineated by contours labeled with depth measurements. These lines eliminate edge fluting and make each field a more coherent whole, minimizing within-field visual variation and maximizing between-field differences. Edge lines allow very fine value distinctions, increasing scale precision. Between fields, only the *presence* of an edge is needed, a *thin* line of a color not too distant in

value from the scale itself (at left, 3% and 7% screen tints for ground and for building; at right, exactly the same tints with edges). Note the dramatic effect of the contour here, visually shifting color within the outlined form, sharply distinguishing the building from the surrounding ground. This technique of cartography and graphic design is confirmed by theories of vision, which point out that human cognitive processing gives considerable and often decisive weight to contour information.[15]

← In this map, the color merely delineates what is already obvious. Laid down in broad unrefined bands, the strong colors induce a loss of focus of detail on the entire map, making it something to be read only at poster distance. So much visual excitement, so little data, merely to outline a shape

[14] Wendell R. Garner, "Information Integration and Form of Encoding," in Arthur W. Melton and Edwin Martin, eds., *Coding Processes in Human Memory* (Washington, DC, 1972), 261-281.

General Bathymetric Chart of the Oceans, International Hydrographic Organization (Ottawa, Canada, 5th edition, 1984), 5.06.

Planviews drawn by Pamela Pfeffer, student project, Studies in Graphic Design, Yale University, 1988.

[15] David Marr, *Vision* (San Francisco, 1985), 215-233.

William Henry Toms after Thomas Badeslade, *Chorographia Britanniæ or, A Set of Maps of all the Counties in England and Wales . . .* (London, 1742), plate 18.

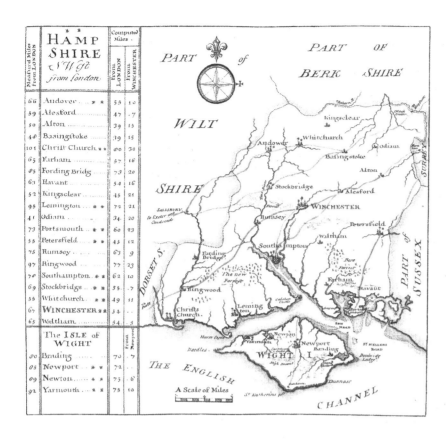

Measured Miles from LONDON	HAMP SHIRE с W & from london	Computed Miles		
		From LONDON	From WINCHESTER	
66	Andover ..... ✱ ✱	53	10	
59	Alesford	47	.7	
50	Alton	39	13	
48	Basingstoke	39	15	
101	Chrift Church ✱ ✱	90	30	
65	Farham	57	16	
95	Fording Bridg	73	20	
61	Havant	54	16	
52	Kingsclear	45	21	
95	Lemington .. ✱ ✱	72	21	
41	Odiam .... -	34	20	
73	Portsmouth .. ✱ ✱	60	23	
55	Petersfield .. ✱ ✱	45	12	
75	Rumsey	63	9	
97	Ringwood ...	77	23	
70	Southampton.. ✱ ✱	62	10	
69	Stockbridge .. ✱ ✱	55	.7	
55	Whitchurch. ✱ ✱	49	11	
67	WINCHESTER ✱ ✱	54		
65	Waltham	54	5	
	The ISLE of WIGHT		From Newport	
90	Brading	70	.7	
95	Newport	72	. .	
99	Newton.... ✱ ✱	75	.6	
92	Yarmouth .. ✱ ✱	73	10	

Thomas Badeslade, *A Compleat sett of Mapps of England and Wales in General, and of each County in particular...* (1724), pen and ink, and watercolor on vellum, leaf 35 (recto).

already familiar to most viewers of the map. Boundary lines should be drawn so as to show clearly what falls on which side, essential details lost here in color cross-hatching. The color misses the point.

The map at left is an unsuccessful imitation of the beautiful original above, translucently aglow with delicate light. Outer areas are given less emphasis, with color gently defining roads, boundaries, and cities. City symbols are marked by red stars indicating how many members each place sent to Parliament in 1724. At any rate, a clear statement about geography, rather than a statement about color.

"ALL things are always on the move simultaneously," as Winston Churchill once described military strategy. So it is also for design and color; even simple visual effects can involve a simultaneous complexity of design issues. For this Japanese textile pattern, white dots produce a slight *contextual color shift* nearby, as in the Albers examples of color interactions. Surrounding the dots and the narrow band of shifted color are *cognitive contours*. And these contours in turn produce a *homogeneous edged field*, a result we have seen both in the ocean map and in the gray tints of the building planviews.

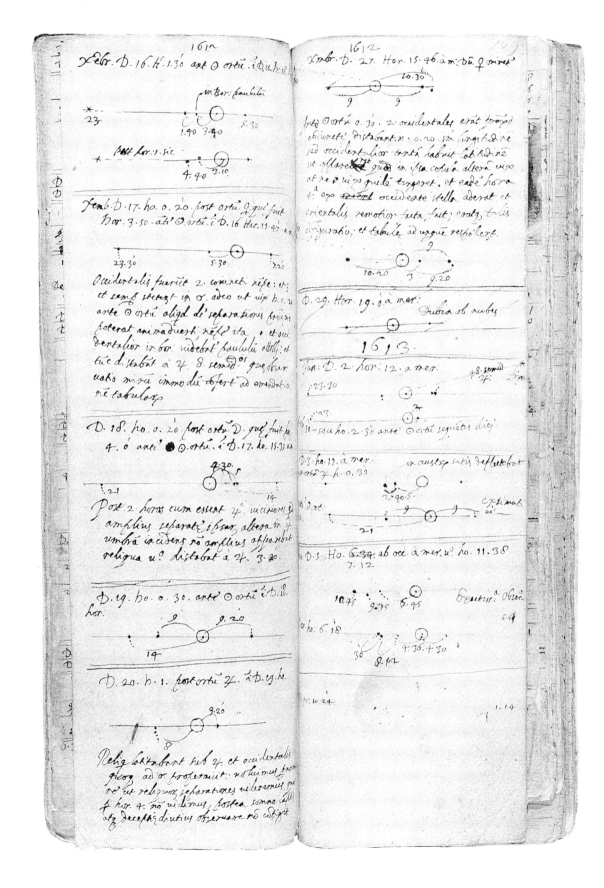

6 Narratives of Space and Time

MANY information displays report on the world's workaday reality of three-space and time. Painting four-variable narrations of space-time onto flatland combines two familiar designs, the map and the time-series. Our strategy for understanding these narrative graphics is to hold constant the underlying information and then to watch how various designs and designers cope with the common data. Examined first are accounts of the motion of Jupiter's satellites, beginning with Galileo's notebooks. Other case studies in our space-time tour are itinerary design (schedules and route maps) and, finally, various notational systems for describing and preserving dance movements.

The Galilean Satellites of Jupiter

On the evening of January 7, 1610, Galileo first turned his new telescope toward Jupiter and saw three small, bright starlets near the planetary disk. His book, *The Starry Messenger*, records the series of observations.[1]

> Though I believed them to belong to the host of fixed stars, they somewhat aroused my curiosity by their appearing to lie in an exact straight line parallel to the ecliptic, and by their being more splendid than other stars their size. Their arrangement with respect to Jupiter and to each other was as follows:

East   ✳   ✳ ◯   ✳   West

> That is, there were two stars on the easterly side and one to the west; the more easterly star and the western one looked larger than the other. I paid no attention to the separations between them from Jupiter, since at the outset I thought them to be fixed stars, as said before.

But either Jupiter or the starlets or both were moving, for next evening a different arrangement appeared. The three starlets were now all west of Jupiter, closer together than before, about equally spaced:

East   ◯ ✳ ✳ ✳   West

Two pages from Galileo's notebooks, recording observations of four satellites of Jupiter between December 16, 1612, and January 5, 1613.

[1] The title page of *The Starry Messenger* reads, "Unfolding great and surpassingly wondrous sights, and offering everyone, but especially philosophers and astronomers, the phenomena observed by Galileo Galilei, a Gentleman of Florence, Professor of Mathematics in the University of Padua, with the aid of a telescope, lately invented by him, on the surface of the moon, an innumerable number of fixed stars, the Milky Way, and Nebulous Stars, and above all in four planets swiftly revolving around the planet Jupiter at different distances and periods, and known to no one before this day, the author recently discovered them and decided to call them The Medicean Stars. Venice. Published by Thomas Baglionus. 1610. With permission and approval of superiors."

At this time I did not yet turn my attention to the manner in which the starlets had gathered together, but I did begin to concern myself with the question how Jupiter could be east of all these stars when on the previous night it had been west of two of them. I commenced to wonder whether Jupiter might not be moving eastward at this time, contrary to the computations of astronomers, and had gone in front of them by that motion.

Galileo awaited the next night with great interest, but clouds blocked his view. Then on January 10, 1610 he did see Jupiter and was able to separate out motion of planet from that of the starlets, a sequence of observation and logic adding up to one of the most important scientific discoveries ever made:

On the tenth of January, however, the stars appeared in this position with respect to Jupiter:

East   *   *   ◯   West

That is, there were but two of them, both easterly, the third (as I supposed) being hidden behind Jupiter. As at the beginning, they were in the same straight line with Jupiter and arranged exactly in the line of the zodiac. Noticing this, and knowing that there was no way in which such alterations could be attributed to Jupiter's motion [alone], yet being certain that these were still the same stars I had observed [before]—in fact, no other star was to be found along the line of the zo-diac for a long distance on either side of Jupiter—my perplexity was now turned into amazement. Certain that the apparent changes belonged not to Jupiter but to the observed stars, I resolved to pursue this investigation with greater care . . .

I decided beyond all doubt that there existed in the heavens three stars wandering about Jupiter as do Venus and Mercury about the sun, and this became plainer than daylight from observations on occasions that followed. Nor were there just three such stars [as I was soon to learn]; four planets do complete their revolutions around Jupiter, and I shall give a description of their alterations as observed more precisely

East   *   ◯ * * *   West

later on. Also I measured the distances between them by means of the telescope, using the method explained earlier. Moreover, I recorded times of observations, especially when more than one was made on the same night; for the revolutions of these planets are so swiftly completed that it is usually possible to note even their hourly changes.[2]

Continued observation soon established that four satellites revolved around Jupiter. Longer time-series, flickering with discontinuities, were plotted by Galileo in 1613 and Cassini in 1668. Satellite motion could be forecast precisely enough to serve as a worldwide signaling clock for determining longitude (since 24 hours corresponds to 360°). Data were entabled—even gridlocked—in ephemerides such as this 1766 *Connaissance des Temps* issued by the Bureau des Longitudes in Paris.

Galileo Galilei, *Istoria e dimostrazioni intorno alle macchie solari . . .* [Welser sunspot letters], (Rome, 1613), illustration of satellites (called by Galileo "Medicean stars" in honor of his patron) following p. 150.

Jean Domenique Cassini, *Ephemerides Bononienses Mediceorum syderum ex hypothesibus, et tabulis Io,* (Bologne, 1668), 34.

Bureau des Longitudes, *Connaissance des Temps* (Paris, 1766), 5.

[2] Translation of *The Starry Messenger* by Stillman Drake, in his *Telescopes, Tides, and Tactics* (Chicago, 1983), 59–63.

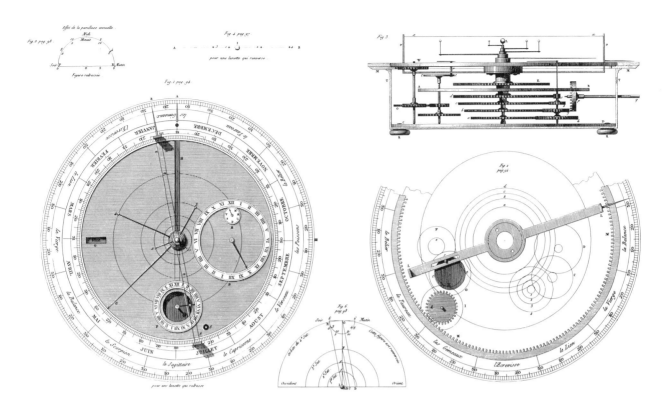

To animate flatland, Galileo and then others constructed Jovilabes, nomogram-like computation devices that recounted orbits of Jupiter's satellites (above). Mechanical models of the solar system in motion showed the interplay of Sun, Earth, and Jupiter, as our shifting vantage point and Jovian shadows masked Galilean satellites from Earth view.

Antide Janvier, *Des révolutions des corps célestes par le méchanisme des rouages* (Paris, 1812), plate VI and plate IV.

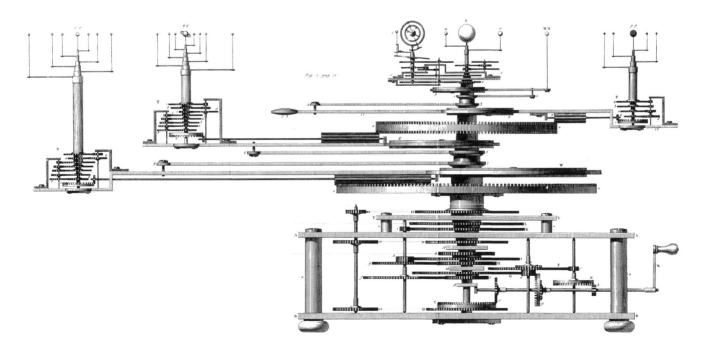

Now, in modern portrayals of Jupiter's satellites, all the individual observations are connected in the corkscrew diagram, with continuous spirals traced out by Io, Europa, Ganymede, and Callisto. These micro/macro diagrams work on a grid of one spatial dimension stretched by time, just like graphical timetables. In our redrawings, the flickering prison bars of the horizontal slices are muted, thus avoiding the clutter of 1 + 1 = 3 effects. It was not until the 20th-century, 300 years after Galileo's discovery, that the dots were linked into continuous curves—an advance in design that came slowly despite the intellectual skills of the astronomers involved. The smooth trajectories of the modern diagram report *every* position of the moons—fitting data for even a few hours of viewing, because of the rapid journeys of the inner satellites. At right is a similar chart for Saturn, including an orbital planview.

Redrawn from: *Sky and Telescope*, 76 (1988); *Satellites Galiléens de Jupiter*, Bureau des Longitudes (Paris, 1987); and *Configurations des Huit Premiers Satellites de Saturne pour 1987, 1988*, Bureau des Longitudes (Paris, 1987, 1988).

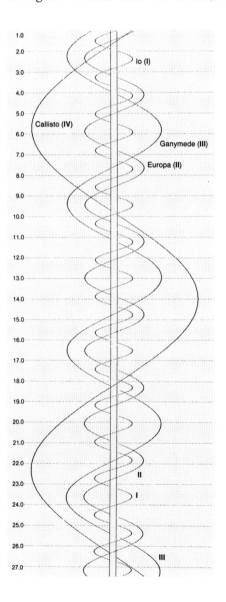
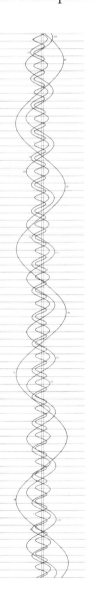
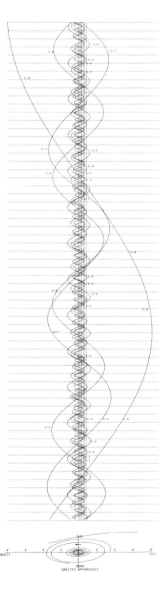

Our story concludes with a new perspective, a very close look at the Galilean satellites. The remarkable 1979 flights near Jupiter by Voyager spacecraft revealed not the luminous pinpoints of reflected sunlight tracing out swift cycles of an elegant and reliable geometry—as had been seen through telescopes for centuries—but, instead, satellites that appeared, frankly, a bit on the lumpy side.[3]

[3] At left, are two inner Galilean satellites—Io (in front of Jupiter) with an active volcano, and, right, the ice-covered Europa. Both are about the size of Earth's Moon; the Red Spot on Jupiter is larger than Earth. At right, a closer view of Io and Jupiter.

Narrative Itineraries: Timetables and Route Maps

Schedules are among the most widely used information displays, with a sheer volume of printed images comparable to road maps, daily weather charts, catalogs, and telephone books. Design efforts for 150 years the world over have yielded some imaginative display strategies. The issues of timetable design are at the heart of envisioning data—large arrays of fussily annotated numbers, thick information densities, type and image together, and multivariate techniques for narrating what is a four or five variable story.[4] And the audience for schedules is diverse, ranging from experts at timetables such as travel agents to those who are not travel agents, an audience of uncertain skills, eyepower, patience.

[4] Among the scant literature is Christian Barman, "Timetable Typography," *Typography*, 5 (Spring 1938), 9-17; Ruari McLean, *Typography* (London, 1980).

A comprehensive narrative description of a transport system requires a record of both time and spatial experiences. Here a complex network of routes is brought together with flight times and identification numbers in a brilliant map/schedule for the Czechoslovakia Air Transport Company in 1933. A playful and polished cover makes the brochure an exceptional union of graphic and information design.

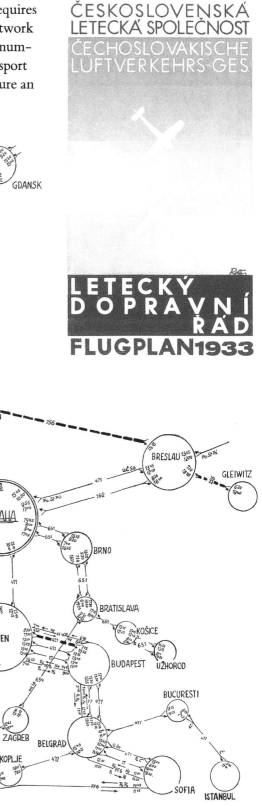

A similar multifunctioning pattern presides over this diagram, a fine combination of flatland and data table. Route map and index, an unusual pairing, are merged in this 200-page timetable for the railroads of China. Although the linework and typography are faltering, the overall layout has a directness and clarity of organization—maintaining the full spatial relationships of towns, patterns usually reduced to a witless alphabetical ordering in a conventional typographical index.

China Railway Timetable, Railway Ministry of the People's Republic of China (Beijing, April 1985), index 4. The numbers along the route lines are page numbers, showing where to look up the detailed schedule for that route.

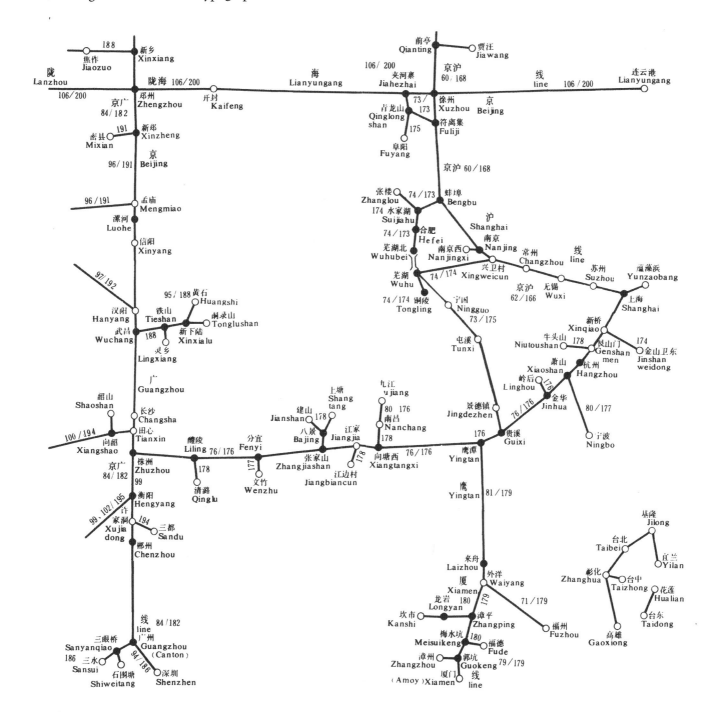

SOME tables are better than others; an example reveals the difference design makes. Millions of copies of this standard typographical table (shown below) have been distributed by the railroad for years. Space is poorly allocated; much of the paper is given over to categories at top that labor incessantly to make only three binary distinctions (between New York/New Haven, leaving/arriving, and weekdays/weekends). All the little boxes create an elaborate but false appearance of systematic order. It resembles the county court house in Vicksburg, Mississippi—a big portico, inflated Ionic columns, with the real work done in back rooms. And so, in this timetable, left-over space beneath the introductory grids and rectangles report on 80 different times of arrival and departure (410 characters). Only 21 percent of the timetable's area is devoted to display of times that trains run. Disorderly footnotes lurk in the basement, waiting to derail insufficiently vigilant travelers.

The most troubling defect of this timetable, however, is the *content* of the information, for the same journey runs no faster than it did 70 years earlier for several trains! At upper right is an antique schedule of October, 1913. Note the wise practice back then of putting names of the people responsible for railroad operations on the cover, a sign of pride as well as an effective force for quality control.

Warren County Court House, Vicksburg, Mississippi, 1858–1861. Richard Pare and Phyllis Lambert, *Court House: A Photographic Document* (New York, 1978), 28.

New York ↔ New Haven Timetable, Metro-North Commuter Railroad, 1983.

NEW YORK TO NEW HAVEN

MONDAY TO FRIDAY, EXCEPT HOLIDAYS

Leave	Arrive	Leave	Arrive	Leave	Arrive
New York	New Haven	New York	New Haven	New York	New Haven
AM	AM	PM	PM	PM	PM
12:35	2:18	2:05	3:45	Y 6:25	8:19
5:40	7:44	3:05	4:45	Y 7:05	8:56
7:05	8:45	T 4:01	5:45	T 8:05	9:45
8:05	9:45	4:41	6:25	T 9:05	10:50
9:05	10:45	T 4:59	6:53	10:05	11:45
10:05	11:45	XT 5:02E	6:33	11:20	1:05
11:05	12:45	XT 5:20	7:08	12:35	2:18
12:05	1:45	X 5:42	7:26		
1:05	2:45	XT 6:07E	7:46		
PM	PM	PM	PM	PM	PM

SATURDAY, SUNDAY & HOLIDAYS

Leave	Arrive	Leave	Arrive	Leave	Arrive
AM	AM	PM	PM	PM	PM
12:35	2:18	2:05	3:45	7:05	8:45
5:40	7:37	S 3:05	S 4:45 H	8:05	H 9:45
8:05	9:45	4:05	5:45	9:05	10:45
10:05	11:47	5:05	6:48	11:20	1:00
12:05	1:45	6:05	7:48	12:35	2:18
PM	PM	PM	PM	AM	AM

The service shown herein is operated by Metro-North Commuter R.R.

REFERENCE NOTES
Economy **off-peak** tickets are **not** valid on trains in shaded areas.
Check displays in G.C.T. for departure tracks.
E-Express
X-Does not stop at 125th Street.
S-Saturdays and Washington's Birthday only.
H-Sundays and Holidays only.
T-Snack and Beverage Service.
HOLIDAYS-New Year's Day, Washington's Birthday, Memorial Day, Independence Day, Labor Day, Thanksgiving and Christmas.

Bold sans serif capitals weak in distinguishing between two directions:
NEW HAVEN TO NEW YORK **NEW YORK TO NEW YORK**

Column headings repeated 3 times and 24 AM's and PM's shown due to folded sequence of times. The eye must trace a serpentine path in tracking the day's schedule; and another serpentine for weekends:

Poor column break, leaving last peak-hour train as a widow in this column.

Too much separation between leave/arrive times for the same train.

Too little separation between these unrelated columns.

Most frequently used part of schedule (showing rush-hour trains) is the most cluttered part, with a murky screen tint and heavy-handed symbols.

Rules segregate what should be together; a total of 41 inches (104 cm) of rules are drawn for this small table.

Wasted space in headings cramps the times (over-tight leading, in particular). Well-designed schedules use a visually less-active dot between hours and minutes rather than a colon.

Ambiguity in coding; both X and E suggest an express train, or even E for Economy.

	4†35	5†00	5x02	5†05	5†08	5†11	5x14	5x19	5†24	5†28	5*33	5x36
New York, G.C.T.	4†35	5†00	5x02	5†05	5†08	5†11	5x14	5x19	5†24	5†28	5*33	5x36
New York, 125th St.	4h46				5h16	5h19	5h22		5h30	5h35	5h39	5h44
Woodlawn	5h00	▲▲	▲▲		✦	✦	✦	✦	✦			▲▲
Mount Vernon	5.05				5.37			5x47		5.55		
Columbus Ave	5.08				5.39			5x49				
Pelham	5.11				5.41			5x51				
NEW ROCHELLE	5†06 · 5.16				5.45	5h42		5x55		6.01		
Larchmont Manor	5.11 · 5.21				5.46					6.05		
Mamaroneck	5.15 · 5.25				5.50					6.09		
Harrison	5.19 · 5.29				5.54							
Rye	5.23 · 5.33				5.58							
Port Chester	5.27 · 5.37				6.03			5x58				
Greenwich	5.33							6x03		6.06	6.22	
Cos Cob	5.37							6x07		6.10	6.24	
Riverside	5.39							6x09		6.15	6.28	
Sound Beach	5.43							6x13			6.32	
STAMFORD ... Due	5.47			5.58				6x18		6.23	6.36	6x33
STAMFORD ... Lv.				6.02						6.27	6.40	
Glenbrook										6.31	6.43	
Noroton										6.34	6.47	
Darien				6.09						6.38	6.50	
Rowayton										6.41		
SOUTH NORWALK				6.15						6.47	6.55	
East Norwalk										6.49		
Westport & Saugatuck				6.21						6.54		
Green's Farms										7.00		
Southport				6.29						7.04		
Fairfield										7.07		
BRIDGEPORT ... Due				6.40						7.16	6.58	
BRIDGEPORT ... Lv.										7.23		
Stratford										7.27		
DEVON (Naugatuck Jct)				6.51						7.33		
Milford										7.39		
Woodmont										7.46		
West Haven												
NEW HAVEN ... Due			6.41	6.47	7.07					7.52	7.22	

Vertical column notes: "Leave Harlem River 4.45 p. m." — "'Merchants' Limited,' via Shore Line (all Parlor Cars) for which special form of ticket must be purchased. See Note." — "Connecticut River Special." — "Does not run Saturdays." — "Boston Express, Daily, via Shore Line" — "New Canaan Express."

LOCAL TIME TABLE.
BETWEEN
NEW YORK AND NEW HAVEN.
HARLEM RIVER AND NEW ROCHELLE.
STAMFORD AND NEW CANAAN.
SOUTH NORWALK AND BROOKFIELD JC.

IN EFFECT
OCTOBER 5, 1913.
REVISED TO OCT. 20, 1913.

Subject to Change without Notice.

C. L. BARDO,
General Manager,
New Haven, Conn.

A. B. SMITH,
Gen'l Passenger Agent,
New Haven, Conn.

Form Adv. 222.

At any rate, the redesign below eliminates all the assorted convolutions from the modern-day schedule and yields a graceful but unceremonious layout. The numbers, no longer serpentined, are now set in Matthew Carter's Bell Centennial, a telephone book typeface designed for clarity of reading in tight spaces (such as the convenient pocket schedule).[5]

[5] Center for Design and Typography, Cooper Union, "Matthew Carter: Bell Centennial," *Type & Technology Monograph*, 1 (1982). Ani Stern did the initial redesign of the New Haven schedule as a student project, Yale University, 1983.

NEW YORK → NEW HAVEN
Grand Central Station

Monday to Friday, except holidays		Saturday, Sunday, and holidays	
Leaves New York	Arrives New Haven	Leaves New York	Arrives New Haven
12.35 am	2.18	12.35 am	2.18
5.40 am	7.44 am	5.40 am	7.37 am
7.05	8.45		
8.05	9.45	8.05	9.45
9.05	10.45		
10.05	11.45	10.05	11.47
11.05	12.45 pm		
12.05 pm	1.45	12.05 pm	1.45 pm
1.05	2.45		
2.05	3.45	2.05	3.45
3.05	4.45	3.05 Saturdays only	4.45
4.01	5.45	4.05	5.45
4.41	6.25		
4.59	6.53		
x 5.02 •	6.33	5.05	6.48
5.20 •	7.08		
5.42 •	7.26		
x 6.07 •	7.46	6.05	7.48
6.25	8.19		
7.05	8.56	7.05	8.45
8.05	9.45	8.05 Sundays only	9.45
9.05	10.50	9.05	10.45
10.05	11.45		
11.20	1.05 am	11.20	1.00 am
12.35 am	2.18	12.35 am	2.18

(Boxed area note: "Economy off-peak tickets are not valid on trains in boxed areas.")

X Express
• Does not stop at 125th Street

Holidays: New Year's Day, Washington's Birthday, Memorial Day, Independence Day, Labor Day, Thanksgiving and Christmas.

NEW HAVEN ↑ NEW YORK
Grand Central Station

Monday to Friday, except holidays		Saturday, Sunday, and holidays	
Leaves New York	Arrives New Haven	Leaves New York	Arrives New Haven
12.35 am	2.18	12.35 am	2.18
5.40 am	7.44 am	5.40 am	7.37 am
7.05	8.45		
8.05	9.45	8.05	9.45
9.05	10.45		
10.05	11.45	10.05	11.47
11.05	12.45 pm		
12.05 pm	1.45	12.05 pm	1.45 pm
1.05	2.45		
2.05	3.45	2.05	3.45
3.05	4.45	3.05 Saturdays only	4.45
4.01	5.45	4.05	5.45
4.41	6.25		
4.59	6.53		
x 5.02 •	6.33	5.05	6.48
5.20 •	7.08		
5.42 •	7.26		
x 6.07 •	7.46	6.05	7.48
6.25	8.19		
7.05	8.56	7.05	8.45
8.05	9.45	8.05 Sundays only	9.45
9.05	10.50	9.05	10.45
10.05	11.45		
11.20	1.05 am	11.20	1.00 am
12.35 am	2.18	12.35 am	2.18

(Boxed area note: "Economy off-peak tickets are not valid on trains in boxed areas.")

X Express
• Does not stop at 125th Street

Holidays: New Year's Day, Washington's Birthday, Memorial Day, Independence Day, Labor Day, Thanksgiving and Christmas.

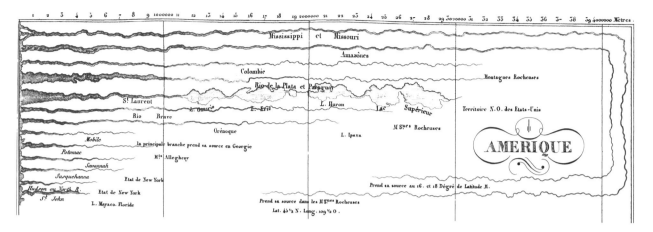

SERPENTINED data formations, like the New Haven timetable, spring up when data collide into a rigid grid. Authentic graphical treasures can result, especially when the data are lognormally distributed as so many variables are. Above, two rivers meander boustrophedonically around a tight frame, weakening comparison of their lengths. And a delight from the 1935 *Graphic Illustration of Tokyo City* (a book too often forgotten), analyzing the water supply system with a very bent bar chart:

Jean Buchon, *Atlas Geographique, Statistique, Historique, et Chronologique des Deux Amériques* . . . (Paris, 1825), no. LXIII. Redrawn.

Tokaido Line at Yokohama Station, Sagami Tetsudo Company, 1985 timetable, 72.

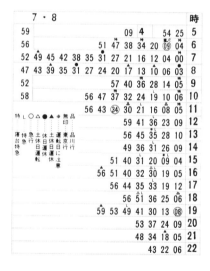

Instituto de Expansão Commercial, *Brasil: Graphicos Economicos-Estatisticas* (Rio de Janeiro, 1929), 17 (above).

Tokyo City Government, *Tokyo shisei Zuhyo* [Graphic Illustration of Tokyo City], April, 1935, 17 (at left).

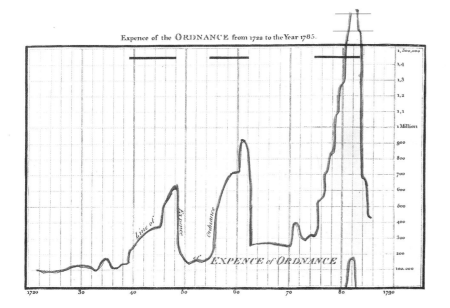

Expence of the ORDNANCE from 1722 to the Year 1785.

Ludwig van Beethoven, *Grosse Fuge in B flat major*, Op. 134, autograph manuscript, composer's version for piano four-hands.

[6] William Playfair, *Commercial and Political Atlas* (London, 1786), text facing plate 34. A failure to deflate monetary units weakens his argument, especially in light of possible postwar inflation.

William Billings, *The New-England Psalm-Singer* (Boston, 1770).

World map redrawn from Kirk Bryan and Michael D. Cox, "The Circulation of the World Ocean: A Numerical Study," *Journal of Physical Oceanography*, 2 (1972), 330.

Airplane schedule redrawn from Edward Tufte and Inge Druckrey, *Communicating Information Visually* (New York, International Paper, 1984).

In this time-series, William Playfair ingeniously spilled outlying data over, first by temporarily extending the grid at top (like ledger lines in musical notation) and then by topologically gluing the data surface from top around to bottom (like octave displacement in music). The result is a torus-graphic. Thick horizontals identify periods of war, when British government spending for weapons multiplied. A ratchet effect appears, as post-war expense fails to shrink back to its pre-war level:

> This, like the three former Charts, is made out from the yearly Accounts laid before the House of Commons; like those, too, it rises in time of war; and has, like them, not returned to its former low establishment. The people, in every different line, are interested in raising the consequence of their department; and example is contagious, when seconded by inclination or by interest.[6]

Playfair's enfolding resembles the gluing of music repeats as well as the visual-musical round at right, a becoming curiosity. Moreover, the 24-hour graphical timetable can likewise be glued end-to-end onto a cylinder, to show a fully connected cycle and to prevent running off the right side of a schedule at midnight. Simply prolonging the grid a few more hours will also show a complete cycle—as in the airplane schedule below, which itemizes a day's visit to Chicago after flying from Atlanta. Globes may likewise be recycled, avoiding ethnocentrism and showing, somewhere in the picture, every country and ocean together in full. →

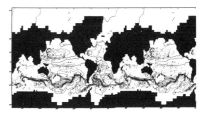

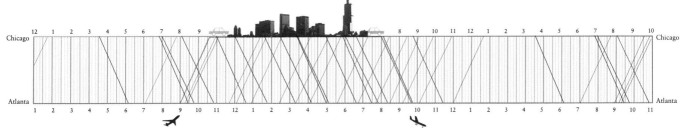

A good alternative to the traditional typographical timetable is the now-familiar graphical schedule. Developed by Charles Ybry, a Paris engineer, the visual timetable provides a detailed reading of times of a particular train along with an overview of the daily structure of times, stations, and routes—separating and combining micro/macro data. Ybry wrote in his 1846 British patent statement:

Invention will be such for each line of railway as to indicate the point of departure and arrival of the up and down trains, and also the bridges or any irregularities on the line or tunnels. It will be evident that the engine driver and guards having such time table with them will be enabled to regulate the speeds of the different trains with great exactness, and in cases where special trains are required the diagonal lines of their speed can at once be determined and ruled on the table, so as to enable the engine drivers to avoid all preceding trains which they may have to pass; for by the table the engineers will not only know the speed at which they

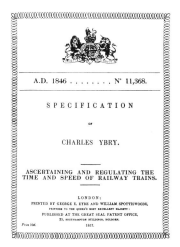

are to move, but they will ascertain at sight positions where all preceding trains ought to be at any moment of time. From the time table shown, a person will readily construct a time table for any particular line of railway, and the same may be engraved and printed, not only for the use of the persons belonging to the railway, but also for the public.

Railways soon came to use the graphical method for planning schedules, especially in negotiating sequences of several trains running on the same line. Today systems of immense complexity are governed by graphical timetables portraying thousands of station stops. We have already seen two fine examples, the Java spy table and the *Shinkansen* master control chart. But Ybry's hope for use of visual timetables by the public has not been realized. On the right, however, is our design of a bus schedule that combines a graphical timetable with a route map overlaid on a precisely detailed aerial photograph, so much richer than the typical schematic diagram of bus routes. Hourly, daily, and weekly rhythms of the buses are clearly revealed, as well as details of each journey. During rush hours, lines densely crowd into spaghetti—but then service is so frequent that the jumble of lines informs the rider simply to show up, for there will be virtually no wait for whatever bus it is that arrives. The gray grid is set at ten-minute intervals in order to ease visual interpolation of the times of arrival. The aerial photograph unveils the area mostly at the level of *house resolution*, that is, with sufficiently fine details to show individual buildings. Indeed, the reaction of those who live in the area is to explore the photograph, personalizing the data, seeking to discover their own residence, school, or workplace. Same picture, but many stories.

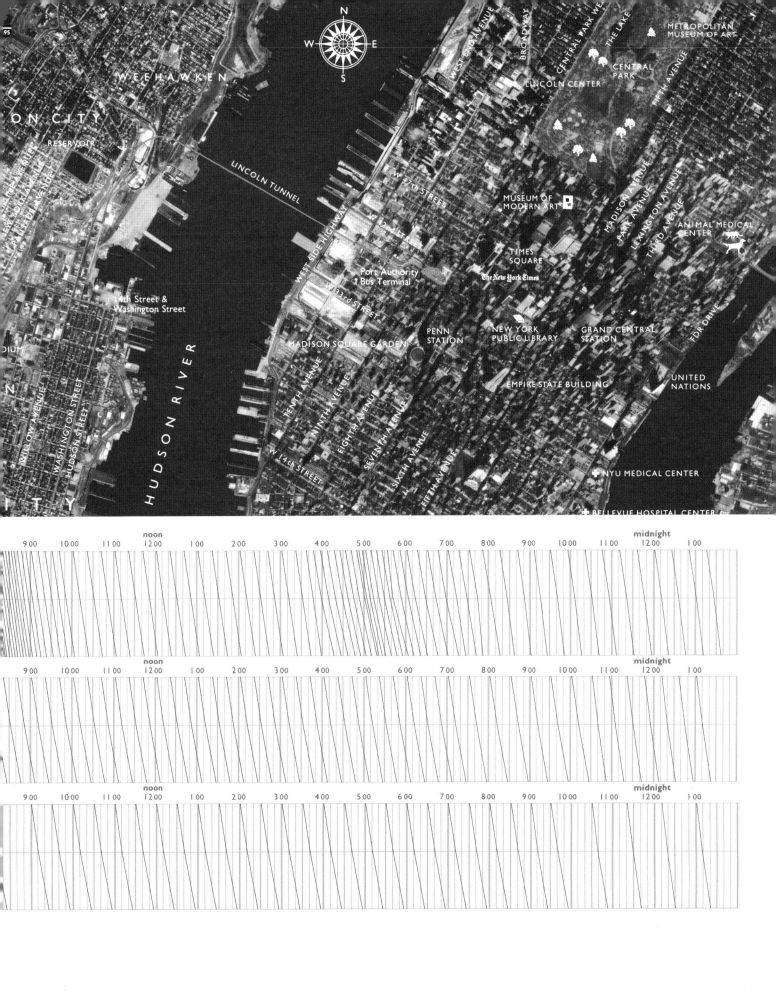

N
W E
S

METROPOLITAN
MUSEUM OF ART

WEEHAWKEN

WEST SIDE AVENUE

CENTRAL PARK WE

BROADWAY

THE LAKE

CENTRAL
PARK

ON CITY

LINCOLN CENTER

FIFTH AVENUE

RESERVOIR

LINCOLN TUNNEL

W 47th STREET

MUSEUM OF
MODERN ART

MADISON AVENUE

PARK AVENUE

LEXINGTON AVENUE

THIRD AVENUE

ANIMAL MEDICAL
CENTER

W 42nd STREET

TIMES
SQUARE

WEST SIDE HIGHWAY

Port Authority
Bus Terminal

The New York Times

14th Street &
Washington Street

W 33rd STREET

PENN
STATION

NEW YORK
PUBLIC LIBRARY

GRAND CENTRAL
STATION

FDR DRIVE

DIUM

MADISON SQUARE GARDEN

N

TENTH AVENUE

NINTH AVENUE

EIGHTH AVENUE

SEVENTH AVENUE

EMPIRE STATE BUILDING

UNITED
NATIONS

WILLOW AVENUE

WASHINGTON STREET

HUDSON STREET

HUDSON RIVER

SIXTH AVENUE

FIFTH AVENUE

I T Y

W 14TH STREET

NYU MEDICAL CENTER

BELLEVUE HOSPITAL CENTER

	noon											midnight		
9.00	10.00	11.00	12.00	1.00	2.00	3.00	4.00	5.00	6.00	7.00	8.00	9.00	10.00	11.00	12.00	1.00

	noon											midnight		
9.00	10.00	11.00	12.00	1.00	2.00	3.00	4.00	5.00	6.00	7.00	8.00	9.00	10.00	11.00	12.00	1.00

	noon											midnight		
9.00	10.00	11.00	12.00	1.00	2.00	3.00	4.00	5.00	6.00	7.00	8.00	9.00	10.00	11.00	12.00	1.00

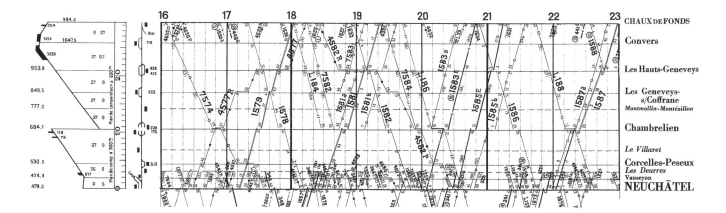

In contrast to the data-rich bus schedule, a Swiss Federal Railroad chart chronicles just a few local trains proceeding daily from Chaux de Fonds in 1932. Note the distinctive pattern here—rhythmic diagonals cross only at stations, indicating that a single track serves the line and, consequently, trains are able to pass one another only at sidings within stations. Visual timetables help plan such passings; it would be clumsy and awkward to design such a pattern nonvisually.

The space-time grid has a natural universality, with nearly boundless subtleties and extensions.[7] Organized like the graphical timetable, this unusual arrangement below simultaneously describes two dimensions, space *and* time, on the horizontal while maintaining a vertical spatial dimension. A complete year-long life cycle of *Popillia japonica Newman* (the Japanese beetle) is shown, transparently, in a smooth escape from flatland brought about by doubling up variables along the horizontal.

Chemins de Fer Fédéraux, Horaire du 22 Mai 1932-14 Mai 1933, I-5.

[7] For the space-time graphs of quantum electrodynamics, see Richard P. Feynman, *QED: The Strange Theory of Light and Matter* (Princeton, 1985).

L. Hugh Newman, *Man and Insects* (London, 1965), 104-105.

[8] Herbert A. Klein, "Condensed Dynamic Images," *Dialogos*, 3 (Winter 1987), 5.

Ludwig Strecker, *Richard Wagner als Verlagsgefährte* (Mainz, 1951), Tabelle III.

Bumps chart of the Oxford University Torpids redrawn from *The Times*, March 3, 1987.

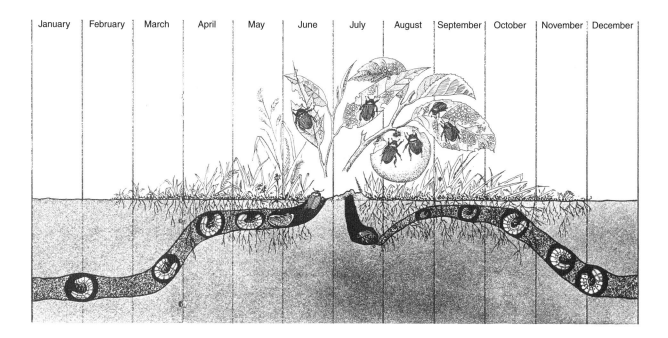

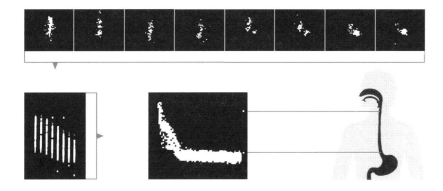

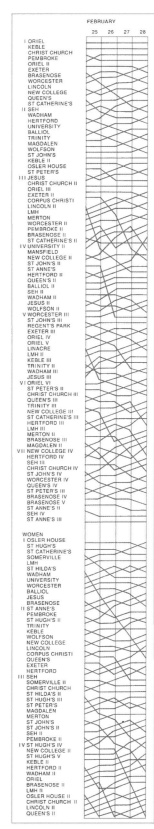

And here is the long-awaited esophageal timetable, narrating movement of food from mouth to stomach. Sequenced images are condensed onto a space-time grid, along with a measure of radioactive intensity:

Eight of the consecutive 0.2 second 64 by 64 standard image frames (top) show radioactive liquid descending to the stomach. The transit process involves only one dimension of the esophagus; lateral motion is of no concern. Therefore, each image frame was compressed into a column one pixel wide by summing the counts along horizontal rows. The columns were assembled in order side by side, including the eight above but totalling sixty in the entire study, to create the condensed dynamic image of an entire swallow (bottom). The horizontal axis encompasses 12 seconds of time, the vertical axis the spatial span from mouth to stomach. The bolus shows uncomplicated downward transit, a normal result.[8]

Also recounting place in time, the engaging "bumps chart" at right tallies results of English collegiate rowing contests. Bumps races come about because the narrowness of rivers precludes more than two crews from rowing side-by-side; in fact on bends there may be room for only one boat. At the beginning of a race, crews are spaced apart at intervals, the starting gun is fired, and they row like mad trying to catch the boat immediately in front. When a boat overtakes another, the crew in front pulls over and the one formerly behind goes on by, now in pursuit of the boat next ahead. In times past, the boats may have actually bumped, signaling a passing and crossed lines on the chart. And, below, a timetable of Wagner's operas, from writing of text and music to first performance.

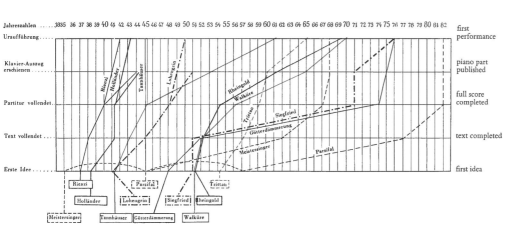

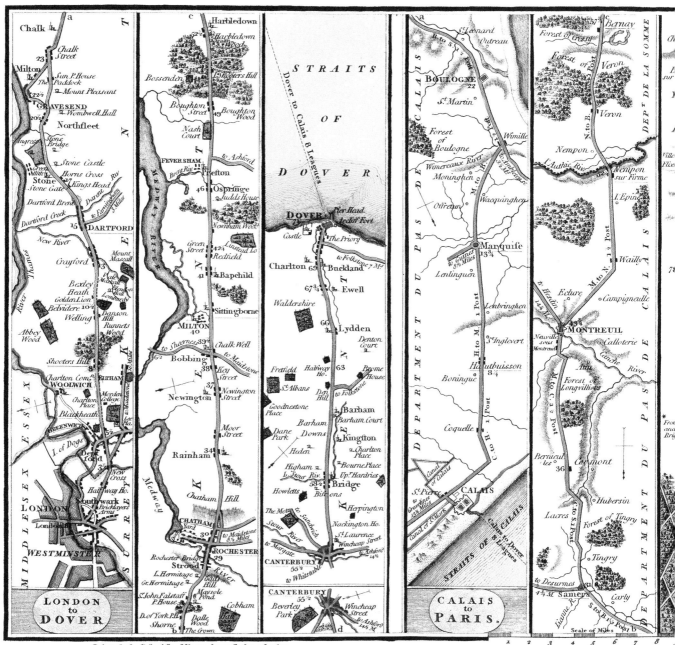

Graphical timetables compress the dimensionality of data by measuring distance along the rail line itself, converting three-space reality into a lineland path on paper, much like the itinerary or strip map. Here is an extraordinary guide, running from London to Dover, across the sea, and thence from Calais to Paris. The route's direction orients each strip, as the normally fixed compass pointer diligently rotates from slice to slice in this *Tale of Two Cities*. Various inns and rest stops are indicated along

A New Plan of the Road from London to Dover, and from Calais to Paris, Charles Smith, mapseller, No. 172 (London, 1801).

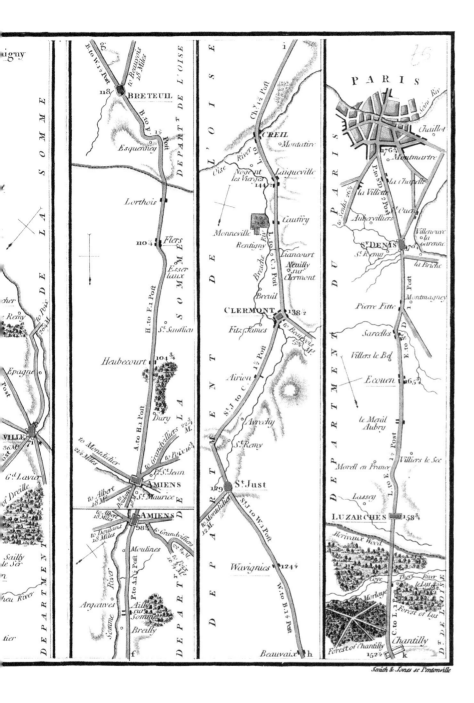

Smith & Jones se Pentonville

[9] On itinerary maps, see P. D. A. Harvey, *The History of Topographical Maps* (London, 1980); and the introduction by J. B. Harley to a facsimile edition of John Ogilby, *Britannia* (London, 1675; Amsterdam, 1970), v–xxxi. Occidental strip maps show roads running from top to bottom with the typeset annotation reading horizontally. In contrast, many 19th-century Japanese tour guides—essentially extended book-length itinerary maps—portray journeys running from right to left, with the verticality of oriental languages conveniently labeling

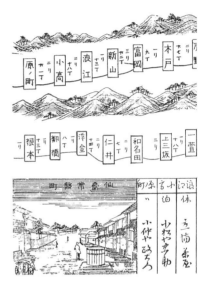

horizontal flow. A sample here from 1868, with places to stay and to take a tea break listed beneath the path. In these guides, the route map is uninterrupted (avoiding the discontinuities of western strip maps), since the book is made from a long thin horizontal strip, gathered and bound up into a continuously flowing set of linked pages. Below, another horizontal path, from a section of Moronobu's 1690 panorama of the Tokaida, the road from Kyoto to Edo (Tokyo):

the muddy journey, which was taken by horses and coach in 1801. Note the two-sided accents on the edges of gridded city streets (as we saw in Chapter 4). Such strip maps, something of a wrong-way departure from flatland toward lineland (it depends on what is done with the second dimension that has opened up), do allow viewers to edit and to focus directly on the relevant—compensating somewhat for loss of context. But what if we were to change our minds in midcourse?[9]

Dance Notation: Commotion and Order

Systems of dance notation translate human movements into signs tran-
scribed onto flatland, permanently preserving the visual instant. Design
strategies for recording dance movements encompass many of the usual
(nearly universal, nearly invisible) display techniques: small multiples,
close text-figure integration, parallel sequences, detail and panorama,
a polyphony of layering and separation, data compression into content-
focused dimensions, and avoidance of redundancy.

Now and again, the paper encoding reflects the refinement of dance
itself—a flowing and graceful line embellished by disciplined gesture, a
dynamic symmetry inherent to both individual and group proceedings.
Moreover, some notation systems engender a visual elegance all their
own, independently of motions described.[10]

[10] Useful guides to dance notation include
Wendy Hilton, *Dance of Court and Theater:
The French Noble Style, 1690-1725* (Princeton,
1981); Ann Hutchinson Guest, *Dance Nota-
tion* (London, 1984), as well as her "A Brief
Survey of 53 Systems of Dance Notation,"
National Centre for the Performing Arts (Bom-
bay), 14 (March 1985), 1-14; corrections, *ibid.*
(June 1985), 34-37.

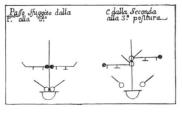

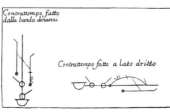

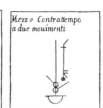

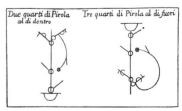

Our understanding of the aesthetics of information is enriched by examining dance narratives and their visual texture. We come to appreciate how the underlying designs bring about and enable the joy growing from the comprehension of complexity, from finding pattern and form amidst commotion. "How beautiful it was then," writes Italo Calvino about a time of radiant clarity in cosmic prehistory, "through that void, to draw lines and parabolas, pick out the precise point, the intersection between space and time when the event would spring forth, undeniable in the prominence of its glow . . . "[11]

Inevitably the texts begin taxonomically, laying out fundamental movements in a visual dictionary of dance elements. For most notation methods, the design of choice is the small multiple—since the analytical task at hand is unswervingly comparative. Variations, sequences, and combinations naturally follow.

Kellom Tomlinson, *The Art of Dancing, Explained by Reading and Figures* (London, 1735), book II, plates IV, XIV, VIII, VI.

[11] Italo Calvino, *Cosmicomics*, translated by William Weaver (New York, 1968), 92-93.

Redrawn from Giambatista Dufort, *Trattato del Ballo Nobile* (Napoli, 1728), 44, 55, 66, 68, 75, 77, 83, and 86.

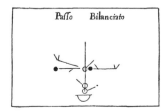

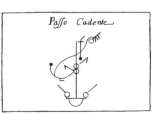

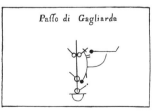

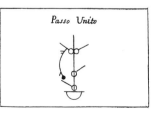

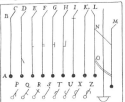

30 TRATTATO
ſcriver le danze, ſtata già da altri ſuf-
ficientemente inſegnata, ma sì ſola-
mente dell'arte del Ballo; ho dovuto
in queſto luogo rapportare quei ſoli ſe-
gni, che ſono opportuni ad intendere
le figure de' paſſi, che ſeguiranno.

La figura ABC rappreſenta il paſſo, di cui A dinota il luogo, dove ſi
trovava il piede prima di camminare:
la linea AB il cammino fatto: e la linea BC il ſito del piede dopo d'aver
camminato, del quale B rappreſenta il
ſito

DEL BALLO NOBILE. 31
ſito del tallone, e C della punta del
piede.
Il movimento piegato ſi deſcrive in
due modi tra lor differenti. Primiera-
mente con una piccola linea appiccata
al paſſo, in giù riguardante, come ſi
vede nella figura D, ed in ſecondo
luogo con una conſimil linea aggiun-
ta al piede, come P rappreſenta.
Il movimento rialzato notaſi parimente così ſul paſſo, come dinota la
lettera E, che ſul piede, come Q, con
una piccola linea all'uno, ed all'altro ad angoli retti congiunta.
Il ſalto è additato dal paſſo F,
a cui ſono due piccole linee l'una al-
l'altra vicine aggiunte ad angoli retti.
Lo ſdrucciolamento vien dinotato
da due linee, la prima delle quali è ad
angoli retti al paſſo attaccata, e la ſeconda ad angoli retti alla prima linea,
e parallela al paſſo, come G rappreſenta.
La caſcata da due altre piccole linee vien dimoſtrata, la prima delle
qua-

32 TRATTATO
quali è al paſſo unita ad angoli retti,
e la ſeconda ad angoli retti ſulla punta della prima caſcante, parallela al
paſſo, ed in ſu rivolta, come H fa vedere.
Il tenere il piè in aria ſi può in due
guiſe ſignificare. In primo luogo troncandoſi con una piccola linea verſo la
punta il paſſo, come dimoſtra I; ed in
ſecondo luogo troncandoſi con una
conſimil linea il piede anche verſo la
punta, come R fa vedere.
Il punto meſſo davanti alla punta
del piede del paſſo K dinota il dovere
appoggiare il piè ſulla punta ſenza
che il corpo vi ſia ſu portato. Ed il
medeſimo dimoſtra il punto meſſo davanti ad un piede, come la lettera S
rappreſenta.
Il movimento circolare adoperato
nel luogo, ove ſi trova il corpo, notaſi
ſopra i piedi con un mezzo quarto di
circolo, quando ſi voglia moſtrare un
mezzo quarto di giro, in quella gui-
ſa che s'oſſerva nel piede T, con
un

DEL BALLO NOBILE. 33
un quarto di circolo, quando un
quarto di giro s'ha a ſignificare, come
ſi vede nella lettera V: con un mezzo
circolo, volendoſi dimoſtrar mezzo
giro, in quel modo, che moſtra X: e
finalmente con tre quarti di circolo,
quando ſono da notarſi tre quarti di
giro, come Z ne dà a diveriere. Quando però dinotar ſi voleſſe il movimento circolare andante, le porzioni di
circolo andrebber meſſe, non già ſul-
li piedi, ma ſopra i paſſi.

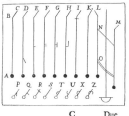

C   Due

On each double-page spread here, identical small-multiple diagrams are repeated, facilitating comparisons among dance steps. Descartes did the same thing in his *Principia*, repeating one particular diagram 11 times. Such a layout makes it unnecessary to flip from page to page in order to coordinate text with graphic. Words and pictures belong together, genuinely together.[12] Separating text and graphic, even on the same page, usually requires encoding to link the separate elements. Within each spread above, for example, attentive readers must repeatedly jump back and forth between text and graphic, which are connected up by 22 letters. Alphabetical labels bestow a sequence on the illustrations, but otherwise are just arbitrary codes, unrelated to the dance movements depicted.

Multiplied consecutive images, below, eerily trace out motion, in these original diagrams from an earnestly scientific system of movement notation. The proliferating cones and plates perhaps help to envision the range of three-space action, although the substance might be forgotten amid witticisms provoked by the eccentric drawings.

Redrawn from Giambatista Dufort, *Trattato del Ballo Nobile* (Napoli, 1728), 30-33.

12 E. N. da C. Andrade, "The Presentation of Scientific Information," *Royal Society Proceedings*, Series B, 136 (1949-1950), 328; Albert D. Biderman, "The Graph as a Victim of Adverse Discrimination and Segregation," *Information Design Journal*, 1 (1980), 232-241; and Edward R. Tufte, *The Visual Display of Quantitative Information* (Cheshire, Connecticut, 1983, 2001), 180-182.

Noa Eshkol and Abraham Wachmann, *Movement Notation* (London, 1958), 10, 11, 20, 31.

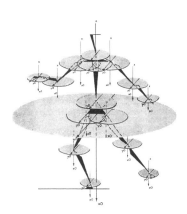

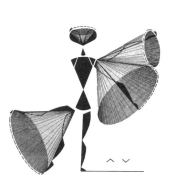

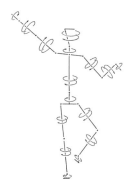

Free play of dance and castanet music is disrupted above by a grid-prison of heavy lines, which clutter the information flow. These active stripes are visually disproportionate to the tiny sum of content conveyed; grids can be implicit or nearly transparent, as a revision below indicates. Note the floorplans of two-space paths of each dancer, and also parallel sequences with profiles of motion running with music:

Shown are redrawn extracts from the score *Cachucha* for the ballerina Fanny Elssler, in Friedrich Albert Zorn, *Grammar of the Art of Dancing: Theoretical and Practical,* translated by A. J. Sheafe (Odessa, 1887; Boston, 1905, 1920), 273; and, below, 31, 34. Read vertically to see the simultaneous actions of four dancers; horizontally for sequence.

De-gridding the procession above enhances the depiction of continuous movement, avoiding the arrested and disembodied quality found in some compilations of dance notation. Here the representations become tiny stick-figures, nonetheless preserving fine details:

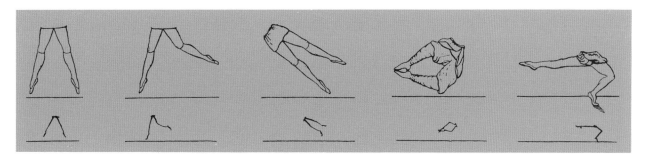

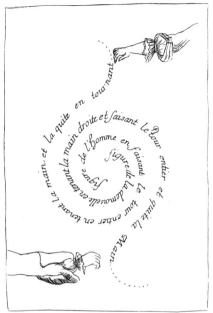
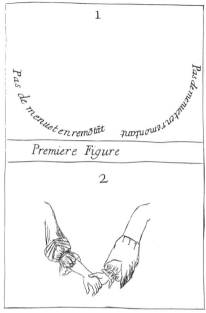

New meaning to the idea of integration of word-and-image is given by these quick-witted drawings from Rameau's 1725 *Dancing Master.* Such innovations, restricted by the exacting horizontality of traditional typographic grids, are now easily—sometimes too easily—accomplished in computerized typesetting and display programs. Rameau furnishes an uncommon demonstration of the *informational*, rather than exclusively ornamental, use of swirling words.

Symbolic abstraction is the prevailing doctrine in modern notational systems, with meticulous codes assembled for thousands of movements in huge dictionaries. Shown are variations on the handstand, as surely must be obvious.

Pierre Rameau, *Le Maître à danser* (Paris, 1734), illustrations 84, 88, 258.

Albrecht Knust, *Dictionary of Kinetography Laban (Labanotation)* (Estover, Plymouth, United Kingdom, 1979), II, 79.

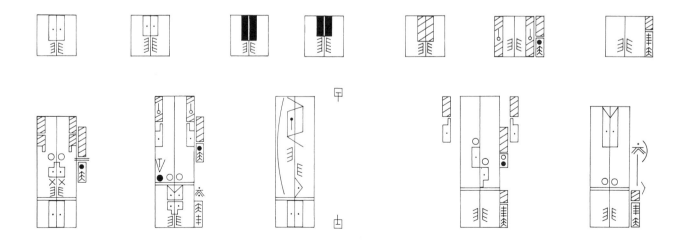

The microscopic and abstracted encodings of contemporary dance notation—so fussy and clumsy and contrary to the wholeness of the substance—provoked the choreographic eye of Lincoln Kirstein of the New York City Ballet:

> A desire to avoid oblivion is the natural possession of any artist. It is intensified in the dancer, who is far more under the threat of time than others. The invention of systems to preserve dance-steps have, since the early eighteenth century, shared a startling similarity. All these books contain interesting prefatory remarks on the structure of dancing. The graphs presented vary in fullness from the mere bird's-eye scratch-track of Feuillet, to the more musical and inclusive stenochoreography of Saint-Léon and Stepanov, but all are logically conceived and invitingly rendered, each equipped with provocative diagrams calculated to fascinate the speculative processes of a chess champion. And from a practical point of view, for work in determining the essential nature of old dances with any objective authority, they are all equally worthless. The systems, each of which may hold some slight improvement over its predecessor, are so difficult to decipher, even to initial mastery of their alphabet, that when students approach the problem of putting the letters together, or finally fitting the phrases to music, they feel triumphant if they can decipher even a single short solo *enchaînement*. An analysis of style is not attempted, and the problem of combining solo variations with a *corps de ballet* to provide a chart of an *entire* ballet movement reduces the complexity of the problem to the apoplectic.[13]

This profound and informed frustration reflects the essential dilemma of narrative designs—how to reduce the magnificent four-dimensional reality of time and three-space into little marks on paper flatlands. Perhaps one day high-resolution computer visualizations, which combine slightly abstracted representations along with a dynamic and animated flatland, will lighten the laborious complexity of encodings—and yet still capture some worthwhile part of the subtlety of the human itinerary.

[13] Lincoln Kirstein, *Ballet Alphabet* (New York, 1939), 49-52, entry on "Notation (Stenochoreography or Dance-Script)." Kirstein describes Kellom Tomlinson's 1735 *Art of Dancing* (which we have seen here and in Chapter 1) as "splendid . . . the finest representations of the Minuet to be found are rendered more complete by a series of careful portrait engravings of dancers moving on the floor-track of a choreographic short-hand."

m'hauer poi col tempo à difdire. E per quefto medefimo rifpet-
to non mi rifoluerei à porre intorno à Saturno altro che quello,
che già offeruai, e fcoperfi, cioè due piccole ftelle, che lo toc-
cano, vna verfo Leuante, e l'altra verfo Ponente, nelle quali
non s'è mai per ancora veduta mutazione alcuna, nè refoluta-
mente è per vederfi per l'auuenire, fe non forfe qualche ftraua-
gantiffimo accidente lontano non pur da gli altri mouimenti
cogniti à noi, mà da ogni noftra immaginazione. Ma quella che
pone Apelle del moftrarfi Saturno hora oblongo, & hor' ac-
compagnato con due ftelle à i fianchi, creda pur V. S. ch'è fta-
ta imperfezzione dello ftrumento, ò dell'occhio del riguardante, perche fendo la figura di Saturno così ◯◯◯, come moftra-
no alle perfette vifte i perfetti ftrumenti, doue manca tal
perfezzione apparifce così ⬭ non fi diftinguendo perfetta-
mente la feparazione, e figura delle tre ftelle; ma io che mil-
le volte in diuerfi tempi con eccellente ftrumento l'hò riguar-
dato, poffo afficurarla, che in effo non fi è fcorta mutazione
alcuna, e la ragione fteffa fondata fopra l'efperienze, che hauia-
mo di tutti gl'altri mouimenti delle ftelle ci può render certi,
che parimente non vi fia per effere. perche quando in tali ftelle foffe mouimento alcuno fimile à i mouiment idelle Medicee,
ò di altre ftelle, già doueriano efferfi feparate, ò totalmente

D   congionte

*Stelle la-
terali di
Saturno
fcoperte
dall'Au-
tore, e loro
condizio-
ni.*

*Diuerfità
nel veder
Saturno
cagionata
da difetto*

Galileo Galilei, *Istoria e dimostrazioni intorno
alle macchie solari . . .* (Rome, 1613), 25.

Epilogue

IN 1613, when Galileo published the first telescopic observations of Saturn, word and drawing were as one. The stunning images, never seen before, were just another sentence element.

Saturn, a drawing, a word, a noun.

The wonderful becomes familiar and the familiar wonderful.

Abbott, Edwin A. 12
Above all, do no harm 81
abstract encoding 27
Adelman, Bob 71
aerial photograph 109
Aesop's fables 65
Akahata [Red Flag] 28
Albers color demonstrations 92-93
Albers, Josef 51, 53, 61, 82, 93
Algonquin writing 73
alphabetical encoding 39
Anderson, Constantine 37
Anderson, Edgar 15
Andrade, E. N. da C. 116
Antropoff, Andreas von 14
Antupit, Samuel 56-57, 70-71
Apelles 19
Appleton, Jay 38
applicant/admit table 29
Aristotle 18, 20
Arnheim, Rudolf 73
Athens 18
Audouze, Jean 23
Avery, Thomas 17
Ayala, Susan 35

back-to-back stem-and-leaf plot 47
Badeslade, Thomas 94-95
Bancroft, T. A. 46
Barême Universe 29
Barman, Christian 101
Barnett, Vic 15, 64
baseball timetable 45
bathymetric chart 91, 94
Beatty, John C. 88
Beethoven, Ludwig van 107
Bell Centennial 105
bent barchart 106
Berlin, Graydon 17
Betrand, P. 67
Biderman, Albert D. 116
Billings, William 107
bird's-eye view 13, 36-38
birds 64
Blake, Peter 34
Bonaduz, Grisons, Switzerland 17
brain electrical activity 78
Bray, R. J. 19
Bretez, Louis 37, 61
Britain 94, 95, 112-113
Brown, Denise Scott 34
Bryan, Kirk 107
Buchon, Jean 106
Bufo americanus Le Conte 14
bumps chart 110-111

Bundesamt für Landestopographie 81
Bureau des Longitudes 98, 100
Burnham, Daniel H. 83
butterfly diagram of sunspots 22-23
Bühler, Paul 62
Byfield, Mary 87
Byrne, Oliver 84-87

Cachucha 117
Calder, Alexander 65
calligraphy 52-53, 65, 68-69
Callisto 100
Calvino, Italo 37, 60, 115
Cameron, Robert 38
Carr, D. B. 17
Carter, Matthew 105
Cassini, Jean Domenique 98
Ch'eng, Ta-ch'eng 76
Chan, Peggy 89
chartjunk 34
chemical elements 14, 39
Chemins de Fer Fédéraux 110
Cheng-Siang, Chen 74, 76
children's shirts 33
China 18, 74-76
China Railway 103
Chinese poets 74-76
Chinese proof of Pythagorean
    theorem 84
choropleth maps 40-41
Chou Pei Suan Chin 84
Churchill, Winston 95
Cigoli, Ludovico 19
clarity and detail 37
clarity of reading 51
Cleveland, William S. 15, 17
clutter 51, 53, 62
cognitive contours 60
color and information 52-54, 58-59,
    63, 80-95
color encoding 78-79
color spots 63, 83
color, multidimensional 88
color, subtractive effects 93
color-deficient perception 93
Colton, Joseph Hutchins 76
computer screens and interfaces 12, 15,
    50, 53, 62, 88-89
computer visualizations 15, 17, 119
Conklin, E. J. 15
context switches. 50
contours 28, 91, 94
contours, cognitive 60
corkscrew diagram 100
Cosmographia 55

Cour-Palais, Burton G. 48
courtroom graphics 31, 35
Cox, Michael D. 107
credibility 32, 34, 50
Cunn, Samuel 16
Cutler, Bruce 31
Czechoslovakia Air Transport 102

dance notation 27, 114-119
De Stijl 87
de-grid design 89
density of information 23, 37, 49-51
DePriest, Douglas J. 17
Descartes, *Principia* 116
detail and clarity 37, 51
Dickerson, Mary C. 14
Dighton Writing Rock 72-73
Discorides 64
Doesburg, Theo van 87
Donoho, Andrew W. 15, 50
Donoho, David L. 15, 50
double-functioning elements 26-27
Drake, Stillman 18, 20
Dreyfuss, Henry 63
Driver, Ann 82
Druckrey, Inge 107-109
ducks 33-34
Dufort, Giambatista 115-116
Durell, C. V. 84

Easton, P. 78
Eddy, John A. 19
Edo 113
electrocardiogram 59
Eliot, T. S. 51
Elssler, Fanny 117
empty space 50
Eshkol, Noa 116
esophageal timetable 111
Euclid 16, 84-87
Europa 100

Feix, M. R. 67
Feynman, Richard P. 110
Fijalkow, E. 67
Fisher, Ronald A. 22-23
Fisherkeller, Mary Anne 15
flatland 12-35
Florentine architects 14
fly-fishing 79
Foley, James D. 89
Fridman, J. 78
Friedman, Jerome H. 15

Gabriel, K. R. 17
Galileo 18-20, 22, 96-100, 120-121
gamma curves 93
Ganymede 100
Garner, Gretchen 90
Garner, Wendell R. 94
Gasko, Miriam 15, 50
Ghizzo, A. 67
Gill Sans 63
Gillen, Larry 31
globes 107
Goldschlager, Nora 59
Gombrich, E. H. 35
Gooch, Frank Austin 14
Goodin, W. R. 28
Gotti, John 30-31
Graham, Gary E. 54
graph paper 59
graphic design 35
graphical timetables 24-26, 45, 107-110
Greenwood, Isaac 72
grid lines 64
grid-square maps 40-41
grove of birches 90
Grün, E. 48
Guest, Ann Hutchinson 27, 114

Hall, D. L. 17
Hampshire 94, 95
Hampton, John R. 59
handstands, notation for 118
Haring, Keith 61
Harley, J. B. 113
Harvey 35
Harvey, P. D. A. 113
Heath, Thomas L. 84
Hellerstein, David 56
Hilton, Wendy 114
Hirata, Kayu 68
histogram 46
Ho, C. Y. 39
Hoboken to New York map and timetable 109
holograms 17
hospital costs 56-57
Huber, Peter J. 15
hue 88, 92
Hurvich, Leo M. 93
Huygens, Christiaan 67
hypertext 15

Imhof, Eduard 58, 62, 64, 82, 90, 93
index design 62, 103
India 58

information density 23, 37, 49-51
information resolution 13, 89
interaction effects 61-65
interface, computer 12, 15, 50, 53, 62, 88-89
International Hydrographic Organization 91, 94
Io 100
Iris setosa 15
Iris versicolor 15
Iris virginica 15
Ise Shrine 13
Israël, Guy 23
Izenour, Steven 34
Izrar, B. 67

Jackson, John 79
Jakle, John A. 38
Jamail, Joe 35
Janvier, Antide 99
Japan 12-13, 18, 26, 28, 40-41, 45, 58, 113
Japanese beetle 110
Japanese tour guides 12-13, 113
Java 24-26
John, E. R. 78
Johnson, David 76
Johnson, Nicholas L. 48-49
jovilabes 99
Judd, Deane B. 93
Julesz, Bela 17
Jupiter 96-100
jury graphics 31

Kana character 68
Kanizsa, Gaetano 60
Keil, John 16
Kellman, Susan G. 31
Kepes, Gyorgy 65
Kessler, Donald J. 48
Kimura, Hidenori 40
King, Henry C. 16
Kirstein, Lincoln 35, 119
Klee, Paul 15, 55, 81, 91
Klein, Herbert A. 110
Klutsis, Gustav 38
Knust, Albrecht 118
Kyoto 113

Labanotation 118
Lambert, Phyllis 104
Lang, Peggy 84
language, vertical 13, 113

Lao Tse 65
layering and separation 52-65
L'Estrange, Sir Roger 65
Leupold, Jacob 66
Lichtenstein, Roy 70-71
Liley, P. E. 39
Lin, Maya Ying 43-44
Ling, Wang 84
Littlefield, R. J. 17
logarithmic scale 39
logotype 21
London to Dover strip map 112-113
Loomis, Elisha S. 84
Los Angeles 28-29, 78
Loughhead, R. E. 19
Lowell, Percival 73

MacSpin 15, 50
Malevich, Kazimir 90
Mallery, Garrick 73
Manhattan 37
Marr, David 17, 94
Marshall, Eliot 48
Martin, Edwin 94
Matsu, sea goddess 76
Matterhorn 81
Matula, R. A. 39
Maunder diagram 22
Maunder, E. W. 22
Mazurs, Edward 14
McGill, Marylyn E. 17
McLean, Ruari 84, 101
McRae, G. J. 28
Melton, Arthur W. 94
Mercator, Gerardus 68
mesh maps 40-41
Metro-North Commuter Railroad 104
Michell, John 73
micro/macro design 36-51, 56-57
Millburn, John R. 16
models, three dimensional 16, 99
Mondrian, Piet 87, 90
Monty, Richard A. 50
moon phases 50
Moore, Charles 83
Moronobu 113
Morris, Margaret 27
movement notation 27
multi-layering 39
multi-window plot 64
multiple-functioning elements 26, 44, 47
multivariate statistical graphics 15
music notation 59, 117
musical accents 82

musical round   107
Müller, J. C.   41

Nathan, Andrew J.   76
nature's colors   90
Needham, Joseph   84
negative space   61-65
Nenka, Kisho   32
Neo-Plasticism   87
neurometric imaging   78
New Haven Railroad   104-105
New Jersey Transit   54
New York, New York   37
New York Times   30
New York to Hoboken map and
    timetable   109
New York to New Haven timetable
    104-105
Newman, L. Hugh   110
Nicholson, W. L.   17
Nishitani, Uboku   53
Nolli map   60
Nolli, Giambattista   60-61
nomograms   99
Notre Dame   36-37, 38

ocean chart   91
Odoroff, C. L.   17
Oesch, Hans   59
Ogilby, John   113
Ohki, Hideo   45
one plus one equals three   53, 61-65, 82
orreries   16, 99

Panofsky, Erwin   19
Papathomas, Thomas V.   17
Pare, Richard   104
Paris   36-37
parts manual   54
Pearson William   16
periodic table   14-15
perspective   14
Pfeffer, Pamela   94
Plan of Chicago   83
planetary machines   16, 99
Playfair, William   107
pocket schedule   105
Pont Neuf   36-37
Popillia japonica Newman   110
population distribution   40-41
postage-stamp designs   67
posterization   35, 50
Powell, R. W.   39

Prichep, L. S.   78
Pridefully Obvious Presentation   16
Primack, Joel R.   48
Pythagorean theorem   84-85, 87

Rafn, Charles Christian   73
rainbow encoding   82
Rameau, Pierre   118
Rand, Paul   34
ratchet effect   107
Rawski, Evelyn S.   76
redundancy   93-94
Rees, Abraham   16
Reynolds, Barbara   60
RGB coding   88
rivers   60, 76-77, 106
road map   93
Robertson, Philip K.   89
Rockefeller Center   36-37
Rome   60
Root-Bernstein, Robert Scott   19
Rosa Ursina sive Sol   21
rotating point clouds   15
ROYGBIV coding   82
Russia   18

Sacre du printemps   59
Sagami Tetsudo Company   46-47, 106
sans-serif type   51
Sapporo   28
Sarton, George   18
saturation   88, 92
Saturn   67, 100
Scheiner, Christopher   19, 21
Schiaparelli, Giovanni   73
Schiavone, James A.   17
Schoolcraft, Henry R.   72-73
Schopenhauer, A.   84
Schove, D. Justin   18
Scruggs, Jan C.   43
sea goddess   76
Sehnal, L.   48
Seibu Railways   45
Seinfeld, J. H.   28
Senders, John W.   50
Senlis   38
serpentined data   106-107
Seuphor, Michel   87
Shea, William   19
Sheehan, William   73
Shibukawa, Ikuyo   33
Shigehara, Hiroaki   45
Shinkansen   45
Shipcott, Grant   84

Shneiderman, Ben   89
Shoucri, M.   67
signals, aircraft   63
Simla, India   58
simultaneous contrast   92-93
Sky and Telescope   100
small multiples   28-33, 64, 66-79,
    114-117
Smith, Charles   112
Smith, Robert   43-44
smog map   28-29, 78
Soerabaja-Djokjakarta   24
Soerabajakotta   24
solar system   16, 99
space junk   48
space-time grids   110-111
spy graphical timetable   24-26
Square, A.   12
The Starry Messenger   97-98
Steinberg, Leo   73
Stella, Frank   12
stem-and-leaf plot   46
stem-and-leaf schedule   47
stereogram   17
Stern, Ani   105
Stiles, W. S.   93
Strawinsky, Igor   59
Strecker, Ludwig   110
strip map   112-113
Strunk, William Jr.   35
subtraction of weight   60
sunspots   18-23, 98
surgeon general's warning   62
Swerdlow, Joel L.   43
Swift, Jonathan   21
Swiss Federal Railroad   110
Sypher, Wylie   26

T'ien Hou   76
tables, design of   35, 55, 56-57, 101-113
Takahashi, Yumi   33
A Tale of Two Cities   112
Taunton River   73
tee-shirts   33
text/figure integration   116, 118
Thomas, Edward Llewellyn   50
Thorfinn the Hopeful   73
The Times [London]   110
timetables   46-47, 54-55, 101-113
Tobler, Waldo R.   41
Tokyo   32, 40-41, 58, 106, 113
Tomkins, Calvin   71
Tomlinson, Kellom   27, 115, 119
Toms, William Henry   94
train lights   68

Treib, Marc 37
Tschichold, Jan 55, 83
Tufte, Edward R. 26, 34, 62, 64, 89, 107, 116
Tukey, John W. 15, 46, 62, 64
Tukey, Paul A. 15, 64
Turgot, Michel Etienne 37, 61
typography 35, 63, 76
typography for maps 62

United States v. Gotti, et al., 1987 31

Valéry, Paul 92
value scale 53, 58, 60-64, 82, 86-94
variation 22-23
Veltman, Kim 14

Venturi, Robert 26, 34, 51
video games 34
Vietnam Veterans Memorial 42-44
Voyager spacecraft 101

Wachmann, Abraham 116
Wagner, Richard 110-111
Walker, Claude Frederic 14
Walker, Gay 16
Wallace, Victor L. 89
Ware, Colin 88
Warren County Court House 104
Washington, DC 43
Watson, James L. 76
weather charts 28, 32
Wegman, Edward J. 17
Wertheimer, Jon 62

Wharton, J. Marcus 59
White, E. B. 35
White, John 14
Windisch, H. 58, 82
windows on computer screens 89
Winogrand, Garry 68
Wright, Lawrence 14
Wyszecki, Günter 93

x-ray films, searching 50

Ybry, Charles 108

Zmaczynski, Emil v. 14
Zorn, Friedrich Albert 117

ARTWORK BY NORA HILLMAN GOELER

CAROLYN WILLIAMS, EXECUTIVE EDITOR, GRAPHICS PRESS

HOWARD I. GRALLA, CONSULTANT FOR DESIGN, TYPOGRAPHY, AND PRODUCTION

COMPOSED IN ET BEMBO, A TYPEFACE BY DMITRY KRASNY

PHOTOGRAPHY BY RICHARD BENSON, RICHARD CASPOLE, ROBERT HENNESSEY, AND GUS KAYAFAS

PRINTED BY GHP ON MOHAWK OPTIONS TEXT

BINDING BY HF GROUP/ACME BINDING COMPANY

DESIGNED AND PUBLISHED BY EDWARD TUFTE